poëts

Visions Of Adolescence

Edited by Chris Hallam

First published in Great Britain in 2003 by
YOUNG WRITERS
Remus House,
Coltsfoot Drive,
Peterborough, PE2 9JX
Telephone (01733) 890066

HB ISBN 0 75434 120 8
SB ISBN 0 75434 121 6

FOREWORD

As part of our ongoing pursuit to present a showcase of today's best up-and-coming authors, Young Writers is now proud to present its 'Teen Poets' series.

Few periods in life are more turbulent - or more crucial in human development than in the early teens. The struggles and trials faced daily can shape and mould our developing persona as we take a tentative step towards our early adult lives. The 'Teen Poets' series aims to bring these growing tribulations to light, providing a valuable snapshot into the thoughts and poetic visions of the teenage mind.

Visions Of Adolescence offers a selection of these poems, as the young writers within tackle a range of vital issues whilst also sharing with us the lighter side of teenage life. The result is a valuable and stimulating insight into the mind-set of the modern youth, and a challenging read for many years to come.

CONTENTS

The Poems

An Ode To The Teenage Years

Trying to get the right look,
Style, pretty much whatever's in,
Keeping count of the stupid things
I do in a day,
Thinking of something, anything
Interesting to say,
To that gorgeous lad in biology.
Those 'must have' shoes,
The fab jeans (that cost a fortune)
Getting the make-up just right,
No one else goes through these things - do they?
The thing you wish you hadn't said,
At least 12 o'clock before you leave your bed,
But making your choices and staying out late,
So all in all I guess they're pretty great.

Jenny Catterall (15)

The Sphinx

Out in the desert lies the sphinx
It never eats and it never drinx
Its body quite solid without any chinx
And when the sky's all purple and pinx
And the sun ever so swiftly sinx
Behind the hills in a couple of twinx
You may hear a bell that clinx
And also tolls and also tinx
And they say at the very same sound the sphinx
It sometimes smiles and it sometimes winx:

But nobody knows just what it thinx.

David Harris (13)

MUM!

Her long dark hair, sleek and straight,
She's always moaning about her weight,
The sparkling fun always in her eyes,
There's nothing about her I despise.
Always trying to embarrass me,
Showing pictures of when I was three,
She always comes home with a treat,
And she purrs like a kitten when I rub her feet.
When we shop, we're the glamour queens,
Yet we're also feisty, man-eating machines,
Even when I'm wrong, she feels bad,
When you put us together we're stark raving mad!
She is forever patting at her so-called tum,
But I love her to bits because
She's my mum!

Katy Bailey (14)

UNTITLED

He loves me, he loves me not,
He loves me, why does he not?
I'm so gorgeous, Granny says,
But does he think that way?
He notices me not for in his eyes I tend to fade,
He adores me, not for my eyes aren't as blue as Jade's.
Why do I look like so?
If I only looked like my mates,
If only all girls were tall, blonde and beautiful.
Alternatively if only beauty is skin deep,
I know my prince and I shall live
Happily ever after. Yes!
He loves me, he loves me truly.

Bintou Magassy-Sabally (15)

First Crush

Oh my god, there he is,
All the girls know where he sits,
The cutest boy in school,
Even though he's not that tall.
Dark and dreamy eyes he has,
But to him all I am is sad,
Popular he may be,
Only me I wish he'd see,
At football he is good,
But classes he never understood.
By him I want to be noticed,
To talk to him I need a motive,
Always he will be my first crush,
But still whenever I look at him, I turn to mush.

Tracy Shrubb (15)

My Feelings

School's boring,
Only nine months left.
I'm hating every minute,
As I can only think of
The tests and the grades.
If I don't do well
My dreams are gone.
If I do do well
My dreams have just begun.
All I want to do
Is sing, dance and act.
But I can't do that
Without those
All important GCSEs.

Christopher Thompson (15)

GETTING A JOB

Make the most of teenage life
Because soon it will be gone,
You will let go of freedom,
Lack of responsibility will go,
Things will suddenly change around you.
You'll enter the never-ending maze of grown-up life,
Always trying to find your way
Though the hard times that get thrown at you
You must overcome,
To be more stronger than before
To open more opportunity doors,
You will start down at the bottom
But soon work your way up
It will be confusing,
A different pace of life,
But all this you must work through
To live the life you want.
None of this will happen though, if you don't get those grades
To prepare you for your future ways
And your first step into the maze.

Karen Stacey (15)

TODAY'S THE DAY

Today's the day,
I'm going to be a bird flying high,
No more nervousness, no more falling,
Everything is perfect,
I love life, everyone's on my side,
Even God,
Today's the day.

Rhiannon Walters (14)

Homeless

As you lie on the streets awake at night,
Cold, wet and awake from fright,
As you are in the dark; cold and alone,
Thinking what it would be like back at home.

As you lie on the streets thinking what went wrong,
Scraping the bits of food you left on your teeth
With your tongue,
Wishing, wondering, why me? Why me?
Thinking why did it have to happen to me?

As you lie on the streets thinking where's your next meal?
Stomach rumbling, you don't know what you feel,
Singing songs to people walking by,
When you ask for money they stop, stare and lie.

As you lie on the streets with no one around,
Watching and listening as you don't make a sound,
As you lie under the stars watching the moon,
Praying that tomorrow will come soon.

Helen Ramsbottom (14)

My Life

My life is full of decisions,
Large ones, small ones,
Full of mixed feelings
That never end.
Full of care that I always share,
My life is with a perfect family,
Full of irritating friends,
I often stop and wonder -
What is life?

Georgina Hitch (14)

Love Is In The Air

Summer is coming and
Love is in the air,
Love is goddam
Everywhere.
Holding hands and
Feeling bums,
Hugging, kissing,
Touching tongues.
Watching sunsets,
Strolls in the park,
Sneaking out,
After dark.
Oh how I wish
For all these things,
If they happened to me
My heart would sing
Aloud with joy
And happiness too,
But what gets me down,
Is my wish won't come true.

Mallory Scott (14)

Just

I want to make you see,
What you're doing to people like me,
Some people look through the bad to the good,
Some people treat people the way that they should.

Is there nothing I can do or say
To make you change your evil way?
To make you feel someone else's pain,
When you put them down again and again.

How would you feel the other way round?
With someone driving you into the ground?
With endless insults flying at you,
Would you still laugh the way that you do?

Maybe you just don't realise,
Maybe you haven't seen tears in their eyes,
Or maybe you do.
Maybe their tears are reflections of you.

Alice Alden (15)

HARD WORK

Being a teen is really hard work,
Where round every corner hormones lurk.
One minute happy, next minute sad,
Then I'm confused, then I am mad.
Sometimes worried about going to school,
Cos I'm bullied by people who think they're cool.
Trying to fit in can be quite hard going,
I'd rather my life was more smoothly flowing.
I hate talking about my growing pains,
Though everyone I know is exactly the same.
Sometimes I'm unable to try and grow up,
I still find it hard applying make-up.
All my friendships have ups and downs,
They all have smiles, they all have frowns.
My social life goes everywhere,
I'm either always at home or I'm never there.
Peer pressure can be troubling,
But I always try and remember one thing,
There's more to life than being cool,
So act like yourself and don't be a fool!

Anya Baldock (13)

School Stairs

It's the stairs that really bug me,
Not the teachers,
Not the lessons,
Not the classrooms,
Not the homework,
But the stairs!
Round the corner there they are,
Everywhere, just waiting, lurking,
Miserable, cold and empty,
Here I am standing at the bottom of . . .
All these stairs!
1 step . . . 2 step . . . 3 step, 4,
Running up and down them,
Sometimes crowded, sometimes empty,
I don't care if it's Monday or Friday,
But they bug me,
All these stairs.

Andrew Cain (13)

The Prisoner

I love this room, more than my old one,
It isn't as big, but it's a lot more fun.
I don't get out much, my choice I guess,
But I like it in here, I must confess.

My bedroom's got an en-suite bathroom too,
It's got everything in it, even a loo.
I don't ever want to leave my room,
The very thought of it brings its twin, doom.

I know one day I'll have to leave it,
Say goodbye when they consider me fit.
I'll do all I can to get back to my room,
Even set off a bomb that goes, well, boom.

Rape, stab or kill, you name it, I'll do it,
The least of my crimes will be to hit
And all to get back to this stupid room
Did I forget to mention, I'm in juvenile prison.

Helen Courtnay (15)

OCEANS APART

(Dedicated for my twin sisters in the Navy)

You're so far away, away from me,
Why not come home, home from the sea?
I miss your face, I miss your smile,
Oh why not come home, just for a while?
If you can't I will understand,
The pain you're going through,
Just like I am.
I haven't seen you for almost a year,
Why is it so long since you where here?
Now you're gone, who can I turn to?
For help and advice on how to get
Through everyday life?
If you could come home,
Just for a while,
You can stop my pain of missing you,
Just for a while.

Claire McQuarrie (14)

QUICK FOOD

Quick food
Can't be late
Cheddar cheese quickly grate,
In a bowl
Stir or mix,
Add two eggs in a fix,
Snips of chives,
Or parsley too
Your must add to the sticky goo,
Then heat it up in a pan
For five minutes if you can,
Without getting too late
This omelette is quick
And it tastes great.

Pippa Hinchliffe (14)

PEACE

Let there be peace.
Let there be peace in the world
And the world will be peaceful.
Let there be peace among nations
And there will be peace on Earth.

Let there be peace on Earth,
Then the Earth will be a peaceful place to live on.
Let there be peace amongst all people.

Peace on Earth amongst all people equals
Social and economic freedom.
This will be true peace to all mankind.

Debbie Soyemi (13)

Half-Term - What A Pain!

'The only thing we have to fear is fear itself',
Said Franklin D Roosevelt.

I had woken up from a terrible dream,
The sounds of laughter and lots of screams,
Later today I would be having it stuck in,
Injections, I'm sure they would sting!

In case you didn't realise now,
I would be having a tooth out,
The worst thing was that it was half-term,
Playing in the park and having nothing to learn.
But now let us fast forward to the time,
When they removed a tooth of mine.

It wasn't so bad at first sight,
Then came in the bright light,
The assistant placed sunglasses over my eyes,
Which was something I didn't despise,
I opened wide and they put in some gel,
Was my mouth going to rebel?

Although I had some tears at first,
They quickly seemed to disperse,
They placed the injection in,
To my relief it didn't sting.
The tooth came out within a flash,
All it needed now was a good clean wash.

I kept it as a souvenir,
Now I didn't shed a single tear,
And now I knew what I had to go through,
Because on Friday they were removing two!

'The only thing we have to fear is fear itself',
Said Franklin D Roosevelt.

Christopher Hayward (13)

BEING FOURTEEN

I haven't done my homework yet again,
I'm dreading my detention with Mrs Renn,
Why are school rules so incredibly mean,
After all, I am still only fourteen.

Last week I tried to get into a club,
I was refused so tried the local pub,
They know I'm underage so now I'm barred,
Going anywhere at fourteen is very hard.

I'm too young for a job with good wages,
So saving up for things takes me ages,
I fell in love with some ninety pound shoes,
Being poor and fourteen gives you the blues.

My best friend just cheated on her boyfriend,
Teenagers' love lives drive me round the bend,
Boys really take their time to ask girls out,
Dating at fourteen is pants without a doubt.

One minute I'm classed as a grown-up,
Then as a kid - make your mind up!
Adult I'm not, kid, haven't been for years,
Being an 'in-betweeny' brings me to tears.

Old people hate any music I play,
They say it was better back in their day,
They fall out with me over Eminem,
Now I'm fourteen I'm not a little gem.

Of course there's a good side to being me,
I don't have to clean or cook the tea,
And nearly every day I see my mates,
So being fourteen is really quite great!

Sally Lamerton (14)

GCSEs

Tick-tock goes the clock,
Each minute that goes by,
A minute closer we get to taking our GCSEs,
This year will pass
And it will pass ever so fast
And before you know it,
I will be sitting down with the exams in front of me.

I still can't believe that it will all be over
In less than a year,
I feel too young to step out into the world
And make all my own decisions,
But I suppose everyone has to,
So at least I'm not alone.

Everyone has been working really hard at school,
Well, almost everyone,
For these exams,
The worst part of it all will be waiting for the results
And the thought of opening my results
Makes me feel nervous, anxious and frightened
And what makes me feel worse is the fact that
These results will affect my future.

When they're finally over,
At least I can plan my future
And decide what I would like to do with my life,
But whether I get good results or not,
Well that depends on how hard I work between now and then,
So what I get in my GCSEs,
We'll just have to wait and see,
Fingers crossed.

Suzanne Eaddie (15)

CANDY

Candy is great, she is so sweet,
Candy is great, she loves licking my feet.

She's always there when I need some care.
She speaks to me, cuddles me, her love is so rare.

Her breed is one of a kind - very hard to find,
She came as a stray on that wonderful day.

She chases cats and yells at dogs,
She's so much fun when she picks up logs.

She can open a door and roll on the floor.
Everyone compliments her and she asks for more.

Candy's not a cat, not a sweet, not a girl with funny feet,
She's not a . . . log?
Not even a hog, but she is in fact,
My gorgeous dog!

Joanne Parkes (13)

MY WORLD

My world is like a roller coaster ride,
There are lows and there are highs,
It's hard being a teenager as many of you know,
Things will come and things will go,
Sometimes you're happy, sometimes you're sad,
Sometimes you're worried, sometimes you're glad,
School is tough, life is rough,
But then you think, you've got
Your family and your friends
And then life's not so hard in the end!

Charlotte Hester (14)

Life Is Fast

Have you ever seen a butterfly flying away,
No bad feeling, no bad thoughts?
Ever thought of escaping and never being hurt,
When you see someone in the street and you say, 'How are you?'
Do you hear the reply?
When you lie in bed do you think about all the
Chores in the day ahead?
Slow down, give yourself a chance.
Life's too short to be unhappy
People who don't stop and whizz through life
Sometimes don't think twice.
When someone dies do you mourn and cry. Why?
Instead think about the happy times and
Laugh at memories they leave behind.
So when the day comes and the candle flickers,
The last note of the music is carried on with you.
Will you have regrets or shame or maybe
Memories you wish to change?
Life is fast, how will you use yours?
What secrets will you unlock?
Life's a mystery.

Rachael Jackson (14)

Tests

It's happening again,
First SATs and more,
Now it's really started -
The dreaded GCSEs.
Not that they're as
Important, as parents
Make them seem.

Ruth Morgan (14)

CROSS AND CONFUSED

What am I, her slave?
I like my room a mess.
She doesn't have to see it,
She's too nosy, she's evil!
She's my mother!

Does she want me to clean her room?
It's beginning to smell,
Not to say about the food remnants,
She's too dirty, she's moody,
She's my daughter!

My music is not too loud,
If anything it should be louder,
He has a problem with it, I don't care,
He's too old, he's selfish!
He's my father!

I don't want to hear her 'music'.
First thing in the morning and last thing at night,
She'll go deaf from it,
She's too stubborn, she's inconsiderate,
She's my daughter!

Zoe Savva (14)

MY MIND

A day in the life of me,
Will help you to understand and see,
How complicated a teenage life can be,
My world is full of friends, boys, fashion and spots,
Parents telling you what's what and what's not,
They try to be cool,
But they don't have a clue,
They're so embarrassing, I don't know what to do.

I'm a teenage girl that likes to flirt,
Share secrets with friends
And dish the dirt,
My life is a roller-coaster ride,
I'm either on the ground
Or on cloud nine,
That's just a taste of my teenage mind.

Natasha Hobbs (14)

The Serial Killer's Mind - Be Careful Girls

Have you got blue eyes,
Or green or brown or grey?
A slim attractive figure,
Delicate in every way.

Do you have blonde hair,
Or black or brown or red?
Is it straight or curly,
Or cropped close to your head?

Are your feet small,
With tiny hands to match?
If they are, come here,
You could be my catch.

Ah, here comes one now,
She's lovely, with blonde hair,
I'll wait till she gets closer,
Then get her out of here.

She really was lovely,
But here comes one more,
I hope she is interesting,
The last one was a bore.

Traci Halsall (14)

Boys Vs Girls

Freak		Geek
Cheap		Cheat
Pink		Blue
Flowers		Football
Chocolate		Cars
Make-up		PlayStation
Fashion		Mud
Shopping		Wrestling
	Fighting	
Punch		Slap
Kick		Whack
Used		Bruised
Thumped		Dumped
	Silence	
Kissed		Hugged
	Together?	

Danielle Smith (13)

My Best Friend

My best friend is very pretty,
Slim, talented and tall,
She's loving, kind and always there,
Especially when I feel small.

My best friend is cool and calm
And she's very caring,
My best friend is very smart,
Witty, blonde and sharing.

We've been best friends for three years
And hopefully forever,
She is the best, best friend to me
And nothing will change that, never!

Sara Jones (14)

Welcome To The House Of Horrors

Welcome to the house of horrors,
Where only fools dare to go,
Go through those cursed doors and you are in for a show,
The bright light draws you in,
The smell is rancid like something dragged from the bin,
Rumours suggest that there is no way out,
You should never have gone in now no one can hear you shout,
Ghosts haunt that evil place,
Look carefully, they have your face,
They circle around you,
You touch them and your hand goes straight through,
They lift you up, you realise you do not have much choice,
They take you through the house and inside each painting,
You hear a different voice,
They show you an empty frame,
You look at your face but it is theirs,
They smile as if they are playing a game,
Next thing you know you are trapped in the frame,
But you have only yourself to blame,
You cannot move as you let out a cry,
When you realise you are trapped you can only ask, why?
So the ghosts wait,
Wait for another to share the same fate,
Welcome to the house of horrors.

Michael Thomas (15)

Just Because

What's wrong with who I am?
Why can't I just be me?
Why is everyone telling me,
The person I should be?

The girl who's deep inside me,
Hasn't changed her ways,
She's still the person that she was,
In her younger days.

Just because I dress this way,
Doesn't mean I'm gone,
My mind, my heart and feelings too,
They still are carrying on.

Even though you don't approve,
It doesn't give you any right,
To always tell me every day,
'You look an awful sight!'

You tell me what you think of me,
Just let your mind go free,
Did you ever think one day,
Inside it would hurt me?

The jeans, the make-up, music too,
I want to be this way,
The person who I am inside,
Is always here to stay.

Becky Green (15)

TEENAGERS

The clock ticks up to midnight,
Your 13th birthday near,
The clock strikes 12 at long last,
Everyone shouts big cheer.

Your blow your candles, 1-13,
Your happiness turns blue,
Who are you staring at in the mirror?
This question puzzles you!

For no reason, at any time,
You seem to want to cry,
Keep asking yourself over and over,
Is it just me and why?

The boy who's been your friend for ages,
Suddenly looks tasty,
Ask him out, he says no,
You shouldn't have been so hasty.

Boyfriends seem to get more serious,
Going out on dates,
Kissing, hugging, holding hands,
Having a boyfriend is just great!

The clock ticks up to midnight,
Your 18th birthday near,
You walk into a crowded room,
Friends and family are here.

Vickie Brown (13)

Growing Up

I started my life when my mum let me out,
I grew up so fast I was soon up and about,
I took my first step at the age of one
And I was walking about out in the sun.
The words just mumble out of my mouth at two
And at three, I was out of my nappies and on the loo.
I started school at the age of four
And crying for my mum, rolling all over the floor.
Five was when I learnt how to read,
At six my writing got into progress but help was in need.
At seven my numbers got involved,
By eight my problems were all solved.
Nine was when my swimming came along,
At ten was now big and strong.
Eleven and this was my last year at primary school,
Twelve and in high school.
Thirteen, a teenager and my childhood is at its end,
So here I am, fourteen and all I do is shop and spend.

Sana Ahmad (14)

My First Crush!

As I walk through the busy corridor,
My heart skips a beat, I could drop to the floor,
Right up ahead of me,
Stands a boy as cute as can be . . .

He stands up straight, a tall six foot two,
His eyes glow a baby blue,
The captain of the football team,
He's the man of my dream.

When I see him I go weak at the knee,
Is this the guy the one for me?
Will he notice me, or will he not?
That's the question I ask myself a lot.

He looks over, I look away,
Will this be my lucky day?
He walks away so cool, no rush,
Is this guy my very first crush?

Nicola Callaghan (15)

MOONLIT DREAMS

Moons and stars of shining,
Fairies and elves of forest,
Are dancing in my head,
                    My head of moonlit dreams.

  Love and hate pour into one
  As we dance to the fire and water
  Beneath the magenta moon of dreams.

Purple skies and pink moons
Centaurs and unicorns
Are dancing in my head.

  Happiness and anger pour into one,
  As we sing to the wind and earth
  Beneath the blue moon of dreams.

Witches and wizards of old,
Dragons and dwarves of gold,
Are dancing in my head.
                    My head of moonlit dreams.

Katy Gaughan (14)

Just One Thing

A pain that comes from deep inside
But you try to push aside
Sharper and sharper, the pain gets stronger,
It stays in your thoughts for so much longer
Is it an injury or is it your heart?
Whatever it is, it tears you apart
From deep within
Underneath the skin,
Only you can feel this pain inside
Yet be so happy on the outside.
You can't share the pain
So your world is full of rain
Some day this pain will fade away
And once again you'll be on your way.
But what will happen when it strikes again?
Will it be easier or will it be tougher?
Will it be steady or so much rougher?
You've been through it once
And had another chance,
Remember one thing
As you sit there crying,
You made it once and are so much stronger,
So don't let this pain last any longer,
Lift your head, wipe the tears
And think ahead to future years,
You can share your joy and share your fears,
Just one thing - forget the tears.

Laura Lomas (16)

I Will Lie In Darkened Corners

I will lie in darkened corners
So I can't see the light of day
Covered by a worn out blanket
I don't need the sun of May.

I wish I could sleep forever
If I was asleep I couldn't rise
To see the bad things all around me
Or see sadness in your eyes.

If the rain's forever falling
If the sun don't shine again
I will rest in darkened corners
Try to fly up to Heaven.

I will try and find some silence
Far away from all this noise
Even in a minute's quiet
My mind at least shall have some joy.

When I look back on past moments
Friends have come and friends have passed
People just don't stay forever
Some friendships weren't meant to last.

If the rain's forever falling
If the sun don't shine again
I will rest in darkened corners
Try to fly up to Heaven.

Mark Alexander (15)

INSTRUCTIONS ON HOW TO COOK YOUR VERY OWN TEEN

Take one small to medium child of 10,
Place in a vat for three years and then . . .
Once suitably aged to the year of teen
Mix gently with mood swings, bad tempers
And a splash of full cream.

Place in an oven and baste it each hour,
With aggression, depression . . . and the juice of an elder flower,
When lightly roasted, place into a large pot,
Let the tantrum simmer for two minutes,
All troubles soon forgot.

Next to the fridge to let it cool down,
When sufficiently cooled, colour will be medium brown,
Add food colouring and seasoning to your preferred taste,
Serve with mixed emotions and . . . cold chicken paste!

Elizabeth Anson (15)

CELEBRATION FOR WILLIAM MAYER AGED 4 HOURS

I have a brand new cousin,
But he doesn't have a name!
I hope my aunt and uncle
Will call him John or Jack or James.
My mother's talking on the phone,
She's talking to my nan.
My father's putting eggs and sausage in a frying pan.
My sister's running round the house,
The dog is eating bacon
And I am thinking,
Wow! What a barmy celebration!

Lucy Sanders (13)

Because Of You

Around, all around, the angels gather,
My dread grows,
As the angry hand of Heaven falls
Against my neck.
It crushes me and darkly
My essence drips,
To the wicked earth
That is my prison.
In my madness I call your name,
While death's shadow
Hovers close,
Now alone, my love falls
Upon blind eyes.

This is because of you.

Sarah Taylor (16)

People

People can be made sad,
People can get mad,
People can be mean,
But people can be kind,
When they need to be.

Some people double cross,
Which makes people more angry,
Some people take the mick out of each other,
Because they're different,
Which makes people's kind side,
Kick and help the person in need,
Make sure you're one of those nice people.

Claire Winney

FOURTEEN

Squeeze, splat? Squeeze, splat?
I've never seen a spot as big as that,
My body has matured,
My chest has grown,
My voice is now a different tone.

The shoes I wear cripple my feet,
But I need them
In case there are boys to meet,
All my family laugh about the tissue
Down my bra, if only they knew,
But they are wrong by far.

My life is very difficult,
My school work is extremely hard
And this year I never even got,
One single Valentine's card.

Don't let me be fourteen for long I pray,
I hope to be twenty-one some day
And I will treat all teenagers with care
And not tease them about the size
Of their underwear.

Amy Caddick (15)

SEASONS

The sun has melted the frost away
Winter is over, it's plain to see,
Tufts of pretty pink emerge on the trees.

Summer is here,
The sun is bright,
Flowers bloom,
The beach beckons.

Whistling winds, golden leaves,
Conkers and acorns,
Autumn has arrived.

Snowflakes fall, it's bitterly cold,
Trees stand bare,
Winter is upon us.

Jennifer Bentley

The Black Side Of Emotion

Another, the fuel for the fire within,
The anger burns beneath the skin,
The mind goes numb, all thinking stops,
Your eyes are blinded by your wrath.

Searching wildly, here and there,
Searching for something you doubt is there:
Something familiar in this world of change;
Something that does not seem to be strange.

Black and huge, the growing chasm
Sends your body into spasm.
Numbed by loss, the eyes now see
Nothing good: an empty infinity.

You look out on a barren land,
No tower of strength to help you stand,
Your lonely mind questioning this:
Do they not me, as I them, miss?

Eyes: mirrors to the soul within,
They tell of life beneath the skin,
Emotion pouring out them through,
I share my pain: share it with you.

Rich Rabone (14)

ALONE

This girl I know so strange but true,
Always feeling down and blue
How could anyone cause so much pain
And abandon such sweetness out in the rain?
Her body scarred and drained of colour,
She never even got to know her brother.
She lost him in a car crash when he was six months old,
But still I see her standing bold.
In a way and look in admiration,
This girl she seems to have so much determination.
I can truly see this girl is hurting,
But still people walk by without even caring.
Even her mum, who drank all night,
Who thought she could solve everything in a fight.
And yes it was her mum who killed her brother
And yes her mum who left her stranded in the rain
And couldn't even begin to imagine the pain.
But still this girl walks on with her head held high
And walks away from the life she had without even
saying one goodbye
Until she couldn't hide her bravery no longer
And collapsed on the floor and said, 'I surrender!'
For if there was a God he would not do this to her,
The pain had become too much to bear,
Not one single person seemed to care.
This sweet girl was stripped of her life
And had suffered so much pain and strife
And from this point on, she realised she was. Alone.

Rachel Baxter (15)

This Love

It's conquered my soul,
This thing, has devoured me whole.
Yet, inside of me, growing like a flower,
Slowly reducing me of all my power.
It's penetrated and altered every last aspect of me
And, induced reconstruction from how I used to be.
This thing, complete with complexity, is truly well designed,
Because somehow I surrendered to total manipulation of my mind.
This. My air, my heartbeat, my blood flow.
And yet, its intentions I could never know.
It's origin, possibly dark,
Exposed to the potential risk to pollute the brain and taint the heart.
Here I am. Captivated by an emotion,
That orders attention and demands undivided devotion.
This feeling flickers inside me like a wild flame,
So hot, so raw and impossible to tame.
My direction, my ability to function,
Unaware I've succumbed to internal abduction.
It stole my senses, holds, unfolds and controls my senses.
Now this thing drowns me, surrounds me and permanently
overwhelms me.
As fresh as youth, tastes sweet like fruit, and undisguised like truth.
My wanted burden, my unsure uncertain.
How do I explain my powerful weakness.
How do I describe this painful pleasure,
This worthless treasure.
How do I describe . . .
This love.

Joseph Rowe (15)

My World

Welcome to my world, please come in!
I guess I should begin by saying that my world is
Far much more than it seems.
My world is a painting, full of difference, colour and inspiration.
There is no black and white, only a spectrum of the rainbow,
Shining with an array of colour.
A smile of gentle friend or foe is my world, that knows not
Of war, darkness and desperation,
Filling the world with much more than a spark.
An open window is my world allowing the wind to blow freely,
Bringing with it a cool breeze that awakens memories of a
Summer once past.
My world is a sonnet much more that fourteen lines,
With all the mystery of the ocean, secrets we will never find.
As the waves slowly roll under the light of the moon,
I sit in silence watching my world from afar, waiting silently to discover
The beauty this world has to offer.

Tarai Makawa (15)

The Creature

He creeps and crawls
In the deep dark hole
He's very much like a tiny vole
Sat up on his two back feet
As if he's upon a very large seat
He creeps around with his nose dug deep
Waiting for a very good sleep
He's the creature that hasn't been seen
He might be mean like a *big* machine
He's the creature from underneath
What's his name, is it Keith?

Stephanie Evans (14)

CONFUSED?

Now other lives are all entwined,
Caution constantly carried out,
If only I could foresee the future,
'Is this the life for me?' I shout.

Emotions have a hold on life
And life's a hold on emotion.
So many questions need answering,
There's no use asking for an answer in an ocean.

There's no escape from reality,
There are routes to be taken.
They say we are at an age,
Where our life depends on decisions taken.

We reply, 'It's our life and we'll live it to the full.'
A reply spoken by too many individuals
And we those individuals,
Are all the same because we're uniquely cool.

Just like so many notes in a bar of melody,
As there are in length of a string,
There is never an outright answer,
For any question we sing.

It's hard to grasp this world as melodic.
But who said we were ready to take on the world?
What would I give to be a child again!
And live my life to a continuous full.

So much contrived confusion,
There will always be people who ponder,
Life goes on, the way we route it,
What does it matter at what they wonder?

Lara Evans (15)

FACE TO FACE

Through the mirror I see a different face,
One with confidence and joy,
Smiling and socialising,
Eyes beaming,
People staring as if the face is amazing.
Inside I'm screaming
But I don't know why.
I'm not pretending to be someone different,
Am I?

I stare a little closer.
How did I ever get to be so grown up?
How did my face ever turn out like this?
It never used to look like this.
Is this me?

You can't tell much about me by my face,
It makes me look like I'm confident and tough.
I might have strength on the outside,
But on the inside, it's mostly fear.
Hopefully it will turn into happiness;
If not,
I'll carry on being two different people,
But which person's really me?

I will never truly know if this is normal
Because I'll never be someone else;
But then again,
Being two people is enough.

Rosemary Pycock (15)

SAVED FROM LIFE'S FIRE (BY THE HEADLAMP OF A CAR)

The light towards me,
Warms the eye,
Clear somehow.
The blinding, fulguration,
The hateful, twisted metal,
Soothing the pain.
Pain, present and awaiting,
Knowing soon I'll fall.
The forest fire rages
(Despite the springs
From my lacrimals* born),
Ineffably blazing -
As is this light.

Yet this scene, mirrored
In the burning wood
Would scorch the flesh
(The smouldering ashes),
Yet pain, I suffer none.
In final blinding moments -
A cold realisation:
Fear I more
The birth to the fire,
Than death,
To the glowing light.

* - Part of eye where tears are formed.

Paul M Chambers (16)

Everyday Life

My name is Liam Lowther,
I don't know what to do,
Someone please help me,
I'm counting on you.
My parents won't stop nagging
And getting on my nerves,
I mean c'mon, won't they ever learn,
Grounding me never serves!
They threw my BB gun in the bin,
Mum's threatening to sell my board,
I keep saying, 'Mum, I'm growing my hair,'
But I always get ignored.
Yeah, my parents can be annoying I know,
But I love them anyway,
If it wasn't for my parents, I wouldn't
Be here today.

Liam Lowther (14)

My Room

My room is a place to retire,
A place to be on my own,
All of my friends are allowed
But it's a strict - no parents zone,
Some things have special places,
Others are dotted around,
Some clothes are in the laundry,
Others are on the ground.
I could stay in there for hours,
Just wondering why,
Why there's green in the grass,
Or blue in the sky?

Ysobel Hallett (13)

Rock 'n' Roll

I like Def Leppard
Judas Preist
Iron Maiden best of beast.

Solo on guitar
The bass loud in your face.
Crashing, smashing, drums are the best.
Put it to the test,
Rock 'n' roll comes from the west.

Ozzy is God,
Lemmy is the Devil,
Now let's push it down to the
Rock 'n' roll level,
It's now or never,
Wear your denim and leather -
Rock 'n' roll forever.

Joseph Johnstone (13)

Snow

Snow falling from the sky,
Landing on heads of passers-by,
Snowball fights, sledging, snowboarding too,
So much for you to do.
A white sheet covers the ground,
Not one bit of grass to be found.
But this all ends,
When the sun decides to send
A ray of light, burning hot
And now the snow is not a lot.

Laura Hyslop (15)

A Farewell

I'm so glad that I've met you
after all these years
but you're going home now
and we're all in tears.

I should've got you something
to remind yourself of me.

It doesn't really matter though
cause if you look you'll see,
that deep inside you'll always find
a little piece of me.

Family are together,
even when apart,
cause there's a little piece of everyone
deep inside your heart.

Katie Jane Leucci (13)

Dolphins

D eep in the sea,
O n the golden sandy seabed,
L ive the most wonderful creatures in the world,
in and out of the sea they leap,
P assing the time however they please,
H igh above the sea they leap,
I magine how smoothly they would glide through the sea,
N othing is as beautiful as them,
S wimming into the sunset as they go.

Suzanne Kimberley (13)

Becoming A Teenager

When I became a teenager I thought everything would change
I thought I would get spots,
I thought I would feel grumpy,
I thought I would feel grown up,
But things have not changed a lot,
I suppose I feel lucky so far.

But sometimes I don't feel so lucky,
Being a teenager can become a bore.
With my mum shouting at me,
What seems like all of the time,
Things seem to become quite a chore.
So then I dream of turning twenty and being an adult,
But then I remember what adult means. Work!
Oh no, I've changed my mind,
Oh why can't I stay thirteen?

Ben Davies (13)

Why?

Why must we all grow older?
Why must time go so fast?
Why must we see our present in our past?
Why? Why?
Why does nothing last, everything is always changing?
Why do people come and go?
I hate that I don't know the answers,
I hate that I don't know why.

Louise Gamble (15)

The World We Live In

Think of Africa,
The sun is burning, stubble grass.
No wind, no rain,
Think of the disastrous word famine.

Hunger hits the body,
Your mouth is dried up, you feel sick.
You feel drowsy, so weak you can't move,
Your cattle die of hunger, no milk.

Everything to you is now a blur,
Everything darkens,
It goes, goes and now it's gone, why?
Because . . .

You are dead.

You've just died of hunger,
It makes you think,
What kind of world are we living in?

Belinda Bal (13)

You're So Not Fair Mum!

'You're so not fair Mum!'
I yell as I storm up the stairs,
Of course she was right all along,
But I don't let that show through my tears.

The very next morning at breakfast,
Everything's fine again,
I wonder how I put up with her,
But secretly think I'm the one who's a pain.

You can't stay out late,
Comes after a long list of rules,
While I'm not listening, thinking about,
How I'll look in my brand new mules.

'She said that she hates me, Mum,'
I sniff as I cry on her shoulder,
I think how much she's helped through my teenage years,
And now through this poem, I have told her.

Elaine Stapleton (15)

FRIEND

I'll be your guardian angel
Looking down from the sky
I'll be your sun through the clouds
Shining from up high
I'll be your shoulder to cry on
When things are looking blue
I'll be your tower of strength
And help to pull you through
I'll be your hope and dreams
And help you to achieve them
I'll be there for you always
Because you are a gem
I'll be there when you're happy
To smile and laugh along with
I'll be there for your bad times too
Because you are a gift
I'll be there for you forever
And never wish to lose
A friend like you is special
And you're the one I'd choose.

Diane Marr (15)

The Pain From Within

You were my necessity
My brother so lovely
An invalid I be
An interval I see
Anonymous I remain to everybody who has forgotten me
My station is right but wrong is the pain I have to plead
War has begun I have to fight to receive my peace
Justice will be shown on my face once the defeat
I thought you were my hope, I thought you were my
strength, I thought your concern about me would never leave
but none of my hopes were true it was all a waste - a dream.

Memories can fade, lies can drown, but the permanent
sorrow will stay a vision incomplete

If you had taken one step towards my heart, I would have
taken a million steps towards yours, however you failed to succeed.

My past I saw was interminable, my present I live is
cadaverously, my future I will see is without your family

What I have written is what you must read, what I have said
is what you must believe.

Sabina Khela (14)

Save The Dead

As the men go to fight,
The ladies pray with all their might.

And they hope that they win,
Cause if they didn't it'd be a sin.

Every man went with pride,
Seeing the dead laying by their side.

The battle raid went on,
As the soldier's torchlight shone.

Every friend suffering,
Shouting something was wrong.

And now I see my friend is dead,
I knew I should have got him fed.

Amit Sahni (13)

IN MY HEAD

Is so much confusion,
My heart is in shreds,
Bleeding for this one person.
My heart is constantly crying,
No one has ever felt this feeling, love.
But when they do they'll know,
Know how I am not being pathetic.
Know how much I hurt inside,
How much I needed to get away,
Anywhere,
The sky was my limit.

But I couldn't do it,
For the people I love who weren't there,
I couldn't let them win.
Win control.
Control over my emotions, my feelings, my life,
I am better than them,
I've learnt from other people's mistakes,
How much you can hurt and damage a person inside,
But I forgive them,
I can help them,
Help them understand.

Kelly Croucher (14)

My Dream

My dreams are myths, legends.
Caught in time by the eye of Heaven.
While I'm flying through a midnight sky,
Prancing unicorns pass me by.

A starry glimpse of a creature so fair,
Breathing in the cool fresh air.
With gracing beauty and great might,
The creature leads me into the night.

A building covered in a misty glare,
I see two cold eyes stop and stare.
Yet, without fear, I move to the door,
Treading with care along the floor.

With a quick sharp howl, my dream takes a bend,
After all, I've been through the beginning, the
Middle and have now reached the end!

Zoë Matthews (15)

My Nan's Dog Holly

Holly is an Alsation,
A very friendly one,
She has her jolly ball,
That makes her all excited.

You can't mention my mum's name,
She goes ballistic,
She'll wait by the gate,
From dawn till dusk.

Holly is the sweetest dog,
So fluffy and cuddly,
Black and brown,
So smooth to touch.

She looks a little fierce,
But wouldn't hurt a fly,
Although she tried to eat a fly,
She's not fierce whatsoever.

Sadie Johnston (14)

WHAT'S THE DIFFERENCE?

Doesn't matter if you're black, white or Asian,
We're all unique, God's creation,
This poem's here to make you listen,
Because how would you feel in my position?
You can be African, Indian or Caucasian,
Any cultures, any sexes, we're a united nation,
As they say, it's good to be different,
It's not about the outside, it's what's within.

There's people from London, Washington, Cape Town
And Dubai,
You won't get to them if you don't even try,
We're all the same, ashes to ashes we die,
I always ask myself, why oh why?
You treat him so strange because he's not from around here,
We're all so different, we should stand and cheer,
My eyes, ears, nose are unique too,
So tell me, what's the difference between me and you?

Romel Davis (15)

Being A Teenager

A teenager's life is the hardest of all,
You're not a child,
But parents think you're still small,
(Or they think you're too wild).

They say as you're older you have responsibilities,
But really they mean there's more work to do,
Then they ask if you've done a certain thing,
Like you've got a clue!

They say teenage years are the best years,
If this is true,
Why oh why
Have we the most work to do?

You're told you should enjoy being a teenager,
But how can you?
You have to work harder at school,
Plus you get tons more homework to do.

When they tell me,
'You've got jobs to do,'
I sometimes feel like yelling,
'Give us a break will you?'

Rowann Baker (15)

Freak

They laugh at you,
Make fun of you,
For a few moments laughter,
But all there is, is tears and pain,
For you to suffer after.

They beat you,
Abuse you,
Just 'cause you don't fit,
I'm not a freak,
I'm just not like you.

Jennifer Dundas (15)

DIFFERENCES

We are the friends of a different kind.
We are not the pinks or the popular.
We are the edges the unpopular.
We don't judge on what you wear or do.
We're the ones you can trust to tell your secrets to.

The music we listen to is of a different kind,
It's more of an expression of the soul and mind,
It's not pop or your rap or tec,
People say it's a pain in the neck.

Popular like for only one reason,
But soon they do their act of treason,
Then they leave you out to the side,
But within minutes we are by your side.
Back to the ground where you belong,
Cos we all have that special bond.

Making your way at school today sure takes a lot,
So family will always be there to get you to the top.
Your friends are there for emotional support,
And will always advise you on that bad report.
To show you how to change those Ds to Bs,
So no matter what stupid things you do,
Your true friends will always be there for you.

Faye Griffiths (14)

SIZE DOESN'T MATTER!

Why am I so small
When my friends are so tall?

I wish that my legs would sprout
Then I would get into 18's without a doubt.

Just last night I went to see Men in Black II,
But I ended up watching Winnie the Pooh.

Because the woman at the ticket booth,
Thought I was young enough to have a baby tooth.

'I'm 15,' I said, but she just laughed,
Which made me go red.

That's why I wish I were tall,
But then again it has its advantages being small.

I can get into places by paying the child fee
And my friends have to pay the adults fee, hee, hee, hee.

Andrew Richards (15)

PRESSURES TODAY

Plastic surgery and dentistry, so much can go wrong,
We've been pressured to be perfect - since we were young.
Liposuction and body piercing, when do we stop?
In music the best looking are always on top.

I saw in a paper a presenter 'wrecked' her mouth,
For corrective treatment she lost her house,
She had a bad dentist crown her teeth,
Is it perfection that we seek?

Her teeth and face are permanently changed,
She's developed a lisp along with her pains,
If she was unhappy then she's worse off now,
From the mutilation that we allow.

No wonder all this beauty stuff sells,
I think we should be happy with ourselves,
But it's hard as teenagers to resist the pull,
Everyone's unique and that makes us special.

Jessica Parker (14)

TEENAGE LIFE

Since I turned thirteen all I think about is boys,
I can't believe that I ever played with toys,
My room is my escape place,
Because I never have my own space.
My friends are really important to me,
Not like fleas.

Round, round is how my head's going,
All my thoughts are flowing,
Nothing's making sense,
I haven't got a pence,
I'm screaming inside,
I just wanna hide.

But I'm gonna have fun,
Cause I don't wanna run,
These years are gonna be great,
Once I get used to it,
I'll just have to wait.

Leann Ingram (14)

TEEN DREAM

What was happening to me was so cool!
I just couldn't believe it!
I was standing there, up on the stage,
I was shaking hands with god knows who,
I was being handed shining trophies and awards of some kind,
I had tears of joy falling down my cheeks,
I was looking at the media taking photos of me, photo after photo,
I was surrounded with friends and celebrities,
I could see guys eyeing gals and gals eyeing guys,
I could hear a fanfare playing in the background,
The feeling at the time was resplendent!
I could see a celebrity advancing towards me with
A red plump cushion covered with a red and golden cloth,
I reached out,
I removed the cloth,
Under the cloth was a key. A car key!
I picked up the key and turned around,
Wow! Wicked! A new Ferrari!
I ran to the Ferrari, I inserted the key into the door,
I opened the door,
I was halfway sitting on the driver's seat and
Guess what?
I woke up,
And found myself sitting halfway on my book and chair,
Holding my locker key in one hand and the cupboard door in the other,
And was looking down at a book, a page full of
equations staring back up at me,
I think that was supposed to be the driver's seat.

Kiran Jabeen (14)

THE WORLD TODAY

Desiring to hurt people every day,
Forgetting that someone bigger and greater sees,
Murder, abduction and pain is their gain,
Sadly forgetting that it ends in poverty.

Gladly seeing people die on 11th September,
Finding happiness in being called a terrorist,
Not seeing sadness when everyone can remember,
How fragile it is to hold on to what you most cherish.

The news is only ever about destruction,
People fighting, children dying,
Children younger and younger are up for abduction,
Lives are lost and families are left crying.

Murders are happening day by day,
Frantic scenes are all we see,
Someone's life lost is another person's gain,
Daily outbreaks of crime and envy.

Houses being engulfed in water,
Valuables in this world being taken away.
Houses with water filling up to half and three quarter,
One can only glance back then look away.

One just wonders how long it will go on for,
Whether or not it will ever end,
Wonder if this is what the world is meant for,
Pray for happiness and an end to the pain.

Victoria Oladejo (14)

ODE TO WRITER'S BLOCK

Damn . . . to staunch the flow
To stop my soul
To quench the will
And hold me close
Fettered with chains of mental links
That putrid smell
This anger reeks
Without a channel
Out of control
Rampaging spirit
Through the black hole
Damn, damn, to douse the flame
Inspiration locked away
Who holds the key?
I do not know
Blocked from my heart
A deadly toll
It cannot flow from mind to ink
Oh anger, rage, that rotten stink!
No words I pen
No song I sing
Shut out from what
The joy should bring
No more, it's sad
So sad, but true
The pen I hold can't write for you
An endless circle - such a bore
I forgot the key before
Emotions tied up in a knot
Oh the dread of writer's block!

Kathryn Castle (14)

What If?

What if there was no hurt?
What if there was no pain?
What if there was no sun?
What if there was no rain?
What if there was no love?
What if there was no hate?
What if there was no fate?
What if there was no happiness?
What if there was no sadness?
What if there was no craziness?
What if there was no madness?
What if there was no dark?
What if there was no light?
What if there was no wrong?
What if there was no right?
What if there was no universe?
What if there was no sky?
What if there was no reason to live?
What if there was no reason to die?
What if there was no boy?
What if there was no girl?
What if there was no oxygen?
What if there was no world?
What if there were no you?
What if there were no me?
What if there was nothing to hear?
What if there was nothing to see?

Well . . .
If there was none of this, then this poem
wouldn't have been made!

Rebecca Fell (14)

What's Cool?

What is in?
What is out?
What clothes can you wear,
When out and about?

In the towns where we are
You must be like the rest,
You must know how to look,
And which brand names are best.

You cannot look different,
You must act the same,
In fact all the fashion
Can be quite a game.

First those shoes are out
And that shirt is in,
But when all that changes,
Those go in the bin.

So what can you do?
Can you change what is cool?
Well, hardly a bit
And that's it, that's the rule.

George Miller (13)

The Empty House

When I came home the other night
I gave myself such a fright!
I knew empty the house would be,
As I searched in my pocket for the key.
I braced myself and opened the door,
Placed both my feet on the hall floor.

I checked the whole of the downstairs first,
Then went upstairs, expecting the worst.
Help, what on earth was that,
Oh thank goodness, it was only the cat!

Kayleigh Copeland (15)

SHADOWS ARE . . .

Shadows are little children
Following you around,
Mimicking your every action.
But when the sun dies away,
They run and hide.

Shadows are actors
They play many parts in one day,
Buildings to birds,
People to places.
They slink away after the play.

Shadows are real people,
Short, fat, long and thin,
Fickle - sometimes there, sometimes
Not.
They deceive you,
Dark and outcast.

Shadows are illusions,
In a kaleidoscopic world,
We cannot feel or touch them,
Yet we can sense one -
Falling over us.

Shadows are . . .
Us.

Tanya Mitra (15)

TEENAGE THOUGHTS

Every day is a war against depression
And I've run out of ammunition.
Now the darkness is coming for me
And I can't help myself with wishing.

We're taught that pain is the ultimate disease,
So why does pain feel like my healing?
Blood, water, I can't tell the difference now,
They're both just fluids with no meaning.

My feelings make no sense to me or the world,
My thoughts dictated by people,
Sexuality is now a toy,
A minority tells us to play.

Are these my feelings anymore?
Won't someone tell me now,
I'm gonna take control of this,
These are my thoughts.

You can't tell me what to think,
You'll never tell me what to think.
Never, never, never,
It's my mind now!

Heather Siddell (15)

THE LITTLE UNICORN

I dream about you little unicorn and wonder if you're true
I wish I could see inside your mysterious mind
What lies behind your lovely eyes,
You're free to roam in people's dreams,
You're free, you're wild, but yet so mild.

You gallop through the mist, your mane dances, it seems alive,
Your magic horn, I catch a glimpse,
I look, I stare, I see your fear, but fear not of me, I mean no harm,
It seems to me, I hear you say, I love to run, I love to play.

Claire Jacques (15)

PAIN IS LOVE . . .

There was this one boy . . .
He meant everything to me,
He was everything and everything was him,
We used to spend time together,
Chatting about us and our future,
But now it's all changed,
This happy feeling that tingled my heart has come to an end,
Now we're like two different magnets that don't attract no more,
We used to be close just like lovers are,
Why have things gone wrong?
I don't like it this way, it's causing me too much pain,
It hurts me like a million pins shooting at my heart,
He used to give me joy and happiness,
I would get butterflies running around my body
When I saw his beautiful face,
This pain runs deep inside and hurts so much you just can't imagine,
Feels like my heart is slowly sinking,
I don't want it this way,
But I can't end this pain alone,
I want things to go back the way they used to be,
I care for him so much more than anything,
These words are coming straight from my heart,
This message goes out to the one I love,
You know who you are . . .

Sharon Sandhu (15)

Growing Up

We're growing up now,
Yeah! Yeah!
Gonna learn to drive
And go to clubs,
I can't wait!

We're growing up now,
No! No!
GCSEs, A-levels, uni, jobs,
So many responsibilities,
What am I going to do?

Growing up,
What can I say,
It can be incredible fun,
But growing up comes with its responsibilities,
Well I guess that's what you call,
Growing up!

Nazneen Tabassum (14)

I'm Going To Be A Star

I just can't wait to see my name up in lights,
No one will stop me, you will all see,
I'm going to go far,
I have great dreams of being a star,
You will all know my name,
All the stars are shining bright,
I know I can reach any height,
Say my name!

Chelsy Holland (15)

DREAMS

Dreams by day, dreams by night,
Any day, any time, even by night,
Some are good, some are bad,
Some are scary, some are sad.

Monsters chasing, cars are racing,
Pigs are flying, dogs are crying,
Cars are bumping, rabbits are thumping,
Objects are jumping.

Happy endings, sad endings,
Adventurous endings, cliff-hangers,
Weird, scary endings,
Time to wake up, up, up, up,
Dream over.

Dreams by day, dreams by night,
Any day, any time, even by night,
Some are good, some are bad,
Some are scary, some are sad.

Stacey Johnstone (14)

UNTITLED

Lunch is over,
We're off to maths,
With pen to paper,
The time should pass.

As I stare out the windows my thoughts stray
As I dream about what I've planned for the rest of today.

Emily Edge (14)

I'M STILL A CHILD

What should I do?
Which way should I turn?
So many decisions to make
And so much to learn.

I want to be successful, reach the skies,
See the pride in my parent's eyes.
But what if I slip and fall?
So much advice to heed,
Being told what I need,
I have trouble remembering it all.

But I'm still a child you see,
Who can't help feeling afraid.
Who knows what I'll turn out to be?
What if I regret the choices I've made?

Who will I meet?
Will I feel complete?
Will I be proud of how I've done?
I keep being told,
It will all soon unfold
And all my worries will be gone.

Karen Davies (14)

MEMORIES

I remember playing with my friends, singing, laughing, joking.
But I will never play again,
Because in this camp there is no singing, laughing or joking.

I remember sitting in the garden under the sun on a summer's day,
But I'll never see the sun again,
Because in this camp, every day is a cloudy day.

I remember sitting with my family at dinner time,
But I will never see all my family again,
Because in this camp one member of my family is with me
And that is God, because he'll never leave me.

Zoe Hyams (15)

MY LIFE

In my life no one listens,
They think I'm a silly fourteen-year-old,
I'm not,
I have feelings,
I sit in my room,
All alone, no one around,
Thinking and sitting,
I just want to scream out,
The four walls around me are closing in,
The room's getting smaller,
No one understands me,
Not friends,
Not family,
I'm all alone with no one to talk to,
I put music on loud,
I want to smash everything around me,
I want to get out,
I'm in my own little world now,
But you have to come back to reality sometime,
I'm back now,
Everything's the same,
No one listens,
No one cares,
And guess what?
It's hell!

Danielle Cook (14)

The Horse Next Door

I see the chestnut beauty,
With the lily-white star,
She swaggers gracefully,
Her hooves clamp the ground.
I touch the silent face,
Her nose warm and silky gentle,
Her hot breath wanders like a dragon's,
Her oak-brown eyes, so deep and big,
Like a Pandora's box of secrets and feelings,
Her coat so soft, shiny, smooth.

One day I had to go,
The holiday encounter to last a lifetime
Sticks to my mind like glue,
Her sight unmistakable,
She's eternal in my memory.

No more soft noses on my sleeve,
No more dragon breath on my icy face,
No more nudges at my empty pockets.

The pain.
The anguish.

Charlotte Button (14)

My Room, My Mess

Clothes strewn about the floor,
Pouring out of every drawer,
Tops, trousers, all my best,
My room, my mess.

CDs lying everywhere,
And in the corner, an upturned chair,
The state of the room, it makes Mum sick,
My room, my tip.

Hairbrushes, magazines galore,
These are the things that cover my floor,
To find a thing's a major hunt,
My room, my dump.

Lucy Littlejohns (13)

What's Your Favourite Pair Of Shoes?

Boots for the walkers,
Sandals for the hippies,
Stilettoes for the party people,
Court shoes for the sophisticates,
Flip-flops for the trendies,
Slippers for the sleepy,
Trainers for the teenagers,
Pumps for the gym types.
All different types of shoes.
What's your favourite pair of shoes?

Red for the bubbly,
White for the religious,
Purple for the extrovert,
Yellow for the cheerful.
Orange for the fiery and tempestuous,
Green for the nature lovers,
Black for the stylish,
Blue for the quiet types,
All different colours of shoes,
What's your favourite colour of shoes?

My favourite shoe is a stylish pair of black trainers,
Fading from black to white with tiger stripes,
How cool is that?
(Though I do like my fluffy pink cat slippers)
How sad is that?

Charlotte Bradshaw (14)

After A While

After a while you learn the subtle difference between holding a hand and chaining a soul,
And you learn that love doesn't mean leaning and company doesn't mean security,
And you begin to learn that kisses aren't contracts and presents aren't promises,
And you begin to accept your defeats with your head up and your eyes open, with the grace of an adult, not the grief of a child,
And you learn to build all your roads on today, because tomorrow's ground is too uncertain for plans.
After a while you learn that even sunshine burns if you get too much.
So plant your own garden and decorate your own soul, instead of waiting for someone to bring you flowers.
And you learn that you really can endure . . .
That you really are strong,
And you really do have worth.

Megha Jain (14)

Sometimes

Sometimes they're nice,
Sometimes they're not,
Sometimes they hit me,
Sometimes they don't,
Sometimes they call me names,
No wait, that's all the time,
Sometimes they stare,
Teachers are all the same,
You've all done it,
So stop it,
It's making me sad
It's making me sick.

Hannah Barlow (15)

Life

I stand at the top of a mountain,
looking out, over the deep velvet blue sea,
the beauty and serenity amazes me,
I'm caught up in the moment,
there are no words to describe how I feel.
Then I realise,
life is like a mountain,
no matter how tired or fed up you are,
a part of you is determined to reach the top,
and once you reach your final destination,
you feel an overwhelming sense of pride and happiness,
that's how I feel,
but I have yet to climb the highest mountain.

Nadia Bailey (15)

Untitled

I'm on the swings in the park swinging oh so high,
Back and forth as fast as I can, I'm sure I can fly,
Bump back down to Earth, he's standing over there,
That boy I like so much with the cool, bright, red hair,
I hope he hasn't spotted me acting like a child,
I want him to think I'm cool, grown-up, sexy and wild,
Better adjust my make-up, brush my high-lighted hair,
Get off this contraption, this child-swinging chair,
Bust just one moment longer, I'm sure he won't see,
I'm enjoying myself so much, just happy being me,
I'll grow up in a minute, as quickly as I should,
I'm not so keen to get there,
You know - Adulthood.

Morwen Chorley (14)

STEREOTYPED TEENAGER

We're supposed to arise at a ludicrous hour
When all of our moods are supposedly sour
We stomp down the stairs at a deadly slow pace
Before reaching the kitchen and stuffing our face
We'll watch the TV for an hour or two
Before just nipping off to go to the loo
Whilst we're in there, we decide to get dressed
We're in there for hours we're known as 'the pest'
Then we finally come out, and it's away with our mates
Or that's an excuse because we're off on hot dates
We stumble in drunk late into the night
And fall up the stairs so we get out of sight
We enter our rooms and fall into bed
And awake the next day with a foul, throbbing head
We come down the stairs and are suddenly surrounded
By our strict, hated parents who tell us we're grounded
But it won't last for long, as we know just too well
That a teenager's job is to make their lives hell!

Quite riled, I get when I hear these things
Of just how much trouble a teenager brings
It's a stereotype that makes me quite sad
Because not every teenager is just quite that bad.

Lindsey Dew (15)

BULLYING

Each comment she makes just fills me with tears,
The more I fight back, the more pain that nears,
Her malicious whispering can be heard,
I struggle to block out every word.

Friends no longer look me straight in the eye,
Whatever happens, I know not to cry,
Nobody cares what I have to go through,
They're just glad it isn't them too.

Tracy Hughes (14)

SELF-PORTRAIT

I picked up the brushes from the floor,
Threw away the dirty water so I could get some more.
Though this time, the painting with others I could not share,
The masterpiece I created did not resemble her.

But it was too good!
I couldn't ignore,
The girl that stared back at me,
I was not sure.

So I took a mirror! And quickly drew
The time ticked by, the hours flew,
Slowly but surely, the canvas turned
Into a creation of me, I learned.

The dark brown eyes,
The curly hair was so fine,
After all effort and work,
The portrait became mine.

At once it was clear and easy to see,
That the painting had always meant to be me!
At last I felt pleased with the image of myself,
It was not of my model but showed glamour and health.

I took one last look, it had been fun,
I put the paint brushes down, my self-portrait was done.

Lisa Edwards (15)

UNTITLED

Clueless of what to write,
A blank page full of invisible words,
A window of opportunity obstructed by me,
My mind is not on this.

Instead it wanders from tree to tree,
In my place,
A world all of my own,
Locked away in my mind.

This place I only visit when I'm troubled or fraught,
It smells of honeysuckle and lavender,
A meadow ripened by rays of happiness,
There is no hurt there, there is no pain.

It lingers like the sweet taste of chocolate,
I am alone sat in the sun,
Free from the world,
Yet not quite from myself.

The sun never sets here,
Sometimes I wish it would,
Then I could leave my haven
And face the things I know I should.

Instead it engulfs me
And I embrace it,
So I am forever locked in this place,
Imprinted on my mind,
Until my fears are over and my troubles far behind.

Emma Hulme (14)

LEAH

(Dedicated to Leah Davies)

If Leah was a piece of treasure
She'd be a diamond ring
Because it brings you so much pleasure
For just a little thing.

Leah was the moonlight
The glisten in the sun
She reminded you wherever you were
You meant the world to someone.

Leah was always full of life
She would always jump and smile
But some days on ward C3
There would be a frown, but only for a while.

Leah lived for seven years
They were seven years of fun
We all loved her so much
Leah, you meant the world to everyone.

On that unforgettable day
No black was allowed
Only Leah's favourite colours
Anything bright and loud.

Whichever star you are up there
You're always the one that gleams
Leah our little princess
Our little fairy queen.

Jodie Cunningham (15)

YOU'RE THE ONE

The first time I saw you
I thought it was a dream
Your eyes were like stars
Flowing clearly like a stream.

You're my morning, my noon and
My Sunday rest,
My song, my moon,
You're the best.

You're everything I need
And more you'll see,
If you hold me close
As tight as can be.

You're the one that I love,
Honour and obey,
I'll do anything for you,
You just have to say.

So when I lay down at night
And feel your breath on my skin,
When you whisper in my ear, 'I love you,'
Feelings of love flow from within.

Once again, you
Whisper in my ear,
'Goodnight, sweet angel,
I love you my dear.'

Emma Jane Mountain (15)

CHANGE AND TRUST

Everyone goes through changes,
Some move away, from the ones they love,
And live with complete strangers,
Others are growing up,
Taking on their future forms,
Changing from a baby,
From a sister or a brother,
From a student to a breadwinner.
Becoming responsible and brighter,
To become a father or a mother,
But changes don't stop there,
They always carry on.
Changing from schools, families or houses,
It doesn't sound much fun,
But some changes can be
Full of bliss and life,
Like when someone receives
Or becomes a wife.
That is one big change,
One that changes the mind.
For trust becomes an issue,
One that closely binds
Two or more people
Together and from then on,
Change and trust
Remain an issue,
To everyone.

Sarita Ramchurn (14)

WHAT'S WRONG WITH THE WORLD TODAY?

An alien came from outer space
To make friends with the human race
He observed the planet for just one day
But as quickly as he came, he went away
And why, you may ask, did his mission abort?
You will see when you read his report:

'On the command of Officer Zarg
I studied these curious creatures
They seemed like us - two arms, two legs,
And the regular facial features.

But when I took a closer look
I despaired at what I saw
A planet so green and beautiful
Was full of poverty, pollution and war.

Some people were living in poverty
But others had money to spare
It upset me that most of the wealthy ones
Wouldn't even share.

One of the most disturbing things
That I noticed here
Were the countless factories, churning out gases
Polluting their atmosphere.

Gunpowder weapons in the past
Ended many thousands of lives
Now there's a bigger threat - nuclear bombs
How long will this planet survive?'

Nicola Crane (14)

My Area

Where people walk, where people talk, where birds swalk,
Multicoloured garages,
Love-filled marriages,
Trees so green,
Mothers so mean,
A building-filled view,
A sky so vast and blue,
Sounds of clatter and banging,
Gleaming white net curtains hanging,
A big popular shopping mall,
PC Plods enforcing the law,
Long lines of slate-tiled roofs,
A street where nothing really moves,
Happy, mad, determined faces,
At night the streets are run with races,
Tall blocks of flats,
Straw welcome mats,
All of us are neighbours,
Some are misbehaviours,
There's a dense green wood,
Filled with ramps and mud,
People with different jobs,
People with different breeds of dogs,
Pigeons diving, swooping, flying around,
New places waiting to be found,
I like living in my area, it's a working society,
A fun-filled area with a lot of variety,
My area is closing up for the night and the
Lamps are illuminating my street,
Come down and take a tour and one day we might meet.

Simon Rees (14)

WRITTEN REFRACTION

The Ice-boy smiles
And drums his frigid fingers
Like light on sound.
He turns
With a frozen flinch,
He walks
Away to the outside in
Glass dome snowstorm
Of the cave mouth.

'It was the straw that
Changed the camel's mind!'
He says, smiling still,
Lips stiller, mouth blacker.
Blacker than the Outside was,
Stiller than his icy gaze.
His gazing, subtly penetrating,
Not calculating - unfazed.

And I dance in the deliquescent
Stillness of it.
Rejoice in its absence.
Find joy in his cold . . .
His coldly bright beguiling stare.

He saw it where I could not.
Where it was, the Ice-boy smiled.
His fugal frigorific, fearless
Face saw, enlightened, conquered;
Then fell, reflecting old-time glory
In the last light of his smiling
Eyes. Frown-less,
In sunset-faded shade.

Ben Mullen (15)

EXAMS

Stressed out?
Must be that time again.
Take a deep breath
And count to ten!
You've revised every text book,
Every note that you've made
And all that you want
Is a well-deserved grade.
You need to relax,
All you can do is your best,
Just learn to keep focused,
As you sit through the test.
Work through carefully,
On each of the questions
And if you don't know the answer,
Make some suggestions!
The exams are finished,
You've been through a lot,
Just the results to come
And you're losing the plot.
What if I've passed?
What if I fail?
I'm sick and tired of
Checking the mail.
It's finally arrived,
But you're holding it away!
You're scared of its contents,
What will it say?

Your results depend on you!
So, do all you can do!

Emily Cornwall (14)

2 Cool 4 Scool?

U go 2 scool,
U got 2 be cool,
U aren't with da crowd,
U aren't allowed.

U don't smoke,
U aren't cool,
U don't drink,
You're a fool.

But they don't c,
That u and me,
Do not freak when they say,
'Geek!'

Cos I don't care
If they swear,
Cos I know dat I'm
Unique.

Gillian Petley-Jones (14)

Life, The Virus

It's surging through my brain
Running in my blood
Causing me such pain
Now nothing can be good.

And yet what can I do?
In what's like a prison cell
The virus is in you too
But you're not bound for Hell.

My heart is freezing ice
But now I couldn't care
Escaping would be nice
But I can go nowhere.

Death, take my soul away
I've nothing left to be
Nothing left to say
Death, let me be free.

Darragh Byers (12)

SUMMER

Periwinkle blue engulfs the cloudless sky,
sun rays beat upon freckled faces,
minds are filled with carefree dreams,
drinking icy lemonade on a white sanded beach.

The familiar scent of sun lotion wafts from sun-kissed bodies,
the murmur of happy voices are as gentle as the lapping waves,
the smell of burgers tickle my nose making my mouth water,
families together enjoying relaxing holidays.

Children playing beach ball, running around in sun hats,
the ice cream man busy selling delicious cones to hungry day-trippers,
tourists exploring the mysterious rock pools,
trying to be the first to catch a crab.

The packed high street filled with bustling shoppers,
trying to find the perfect souvenir,
just complete that image in my mind . . .
summer!

Kate Lowdon (13)

A DAY WITH MOTHER

You're not wearing *that!*
Get in the car,
People can see you!
Stop talking to me,
Everyone will think I know you.
Please get me this,
I really need a new pink jumper.
Why?
I hate you!
Why should I?
Don't be so embarrassing,
You sound *old!*
I don't *want* to try it on!
Not one like *that!*
I'm not difficult,
You're the one who's being difficult!
Can we go home now?
Stop waving at her,
You don't know her.
I *can't* believe you're my *mum!*
Sigh . . .

Sharon Levey (13)

THROUGH MY EYES

When you reach your teenage years,
You start to really see,
What the world is really like,
It's not how you thought it would be.

Looking at present and past,
Getting used to change,
Trying to take it all in,
New feelings can be strange.

It's a cruel world we live in,
Life is one big test,
All your answers don't need to be correct,
You just have to try your best.

We're all trying to grow up too fast,
When life is way too short,
Us teenagers need to step back,
And give someone else a thought.

Laura Cayless (14)

Lost Love

I sit down and think of you, your pretty eyes, your pretty smile
I wonder if you ever think of me too.
I have to smile as I remember the good times we had
I shed a tear as I remember the times I made you angry and mad
So many memories happy and sad, but times with you were never bad
I realise how stupid I was now, but now it is too late
It was my fault, I made the mistake.
I took you for granted and watched you slip by
I really do believe time does fly.
The heartache that I feel inside makes me utter a thousand sighs
Whenever I see you I have to look away or close my eyes
Every time I hear your name I feel unbearable traumatic pain
They all tell me to just try and forget, but I can't
Thinking of you always makes me upset
I try and push you to the back of my mind
But the way to the front you always seem to find
My spine shivers as I think of your gentle touch
I never thought I'd miss you this much
A place in my heart you'll always have
I'll remember you forever
I'll never forget you . . . never.

Dale Peppitt (14)

FRIENDS

Best friends Amina
She's the one who's clever,
Any problems that come her way
She's the first one to stay away.

Best friend Salma
She's the dancing diva,
With the music she turns and spins
Dances and prances until the daylight has vanished.

Best friend Husngra
She's the fashion holder,
Red, blue, green or white
Any colour she would like.
Sequins and beads, diamonds and laces,
She would have them all put on her glamorous dresses.

Lastly best friend Munira
She's the one with the cool imagination,
She would be there if there's someone in need
And everyone would be pleased.

Munira Ghodiwalla (14)

JUST BRINGS YOU DOWN

You know when love just brings you down?
Why isn't there anyone around?
To pick you up each time you fall,
Not even a simple call.

You know when love just brings you down?
Feels as though no one's around,
Heart's aching day and night
And thoughts sometimes bring you fright.

You know when love just brings you down?
Now I'm lost, at once I was found,
Being faced in a different direction,
Knowing we can't be a connection.

You know when love just brings you down?
You don't pay attention to movement or sound,
The world is blank, it seems so far away,
I just can't understand why you didn't stay.

Nadine Tiffany Bourne-Harris (14)

EIGHT LIES ALL PARENTS TELL

At school you have the best days of your lives!
(Books, exams, OK Mum! Alright!)
I'll give you a fiver if you clean the car,
(Then why am I skint then dearest Papa?)

I promise you this is really for your own good!
(I suppose then Mum you must deserve a hug!)
I had to walk twenty miles to school every day
(When asked, 'Don't be silly, it was just round the corner,'
Said Auntie May).

No you can't have another pet, you'll be bored within a week,
(Then why am I the only one who looks after our pet hamster, Squeak?)
If you eat all your carrots it'll help you see in the dark!
(I think I'll just switch the light on rather than messing
About with all that lark!)

You don't need to buy another top, the one you've got is alright.
(Then why don't I have anything to wear for Saturday night?)
Squeezing your spots really will make them worse,
(Better than ten tons of pus hanging on your face like a curse!)

Rebecca Derbyshire (14)

As Time Passes

As moments of time pass by
And past memories begin to lie,
Time grips less each day out of our hands,
When future visions start to land.

No one knows when their time will come,
Others pain forsaken know quicker than some,
Unfortunately one person's time isn't forever,
So why is it that we still can't join, all happy together?

This world that we live in
Brings many unforgiving troubles,
Which writhe in great pain,
Which is untimely and has nothing to gain.

As we look and mesmerise, those amongst us,
Who have many difficulties, illnesses and heartbreaking
Struggles, we stand in great admiration,
On how they forget their own worries and have so much dedication.

Even though they know time isn't forever,
As we all should they grasp all the good things,
Life has to offer
And never say never.

Teisha Ravenscroft (15)

The Teenager!

When you become a teenager,
You start to feel things change.

Your responsibilities become more major
And things feel very strange.

If you think you're very small,
This is like dogs will moult.

You will probably grow up very tall,
Now you've become a young adult!

Chris Newman (14)

MEMORY AND DREAM

Closed eyes, but still you see . . .
Nameless things that don't exist rise with darkness and
fall in the light of dawn . . .
You remember it clearly, but it never happened.
You yell in pain, but you are unhurt,
You see yourself and others die over, but still you all live on.
You met them not long ago, but they do not know or remember you.
You see the same horrible fate over and over,
haunting you, pursuing you . . .
It happened today, but you saw it happen last week.
You were flying, but you have no wings.
You were drowning, but you were not in water.
You were famous, but no one knows you.
Dreams . . .

Some you share with others,
Some only you can remember,
And others remember some, but you cannot.
They make you happy, grievous, sad, angry, distraught . . .
Fragments of remembered dreams swiftly pass by,
Flashbacks of terrible happenings in the past are stirred . . .
You laugh at some, alone or with others, at something
stupid you all did together once.
Memory . . .

Lauren Shaw (14)

Drugs

Eyes shut to the rest of the world,
The depressed addict relieved himself.
His pains fell away from him,
The hazardous pills welcomed him.
They work their evil curses inside,
He knows not what they do.
Their secrets are hidden, unrevealing,
Their identity is kept from him,
They are free.

They speak in the code of death,
They switch on the music inside his head.
A new person is born,
A light, dancing spirit.
His head spins wildly,
He plunges into the empty gloom.
His mourners walking gravely,
From his churchyard grave.

Samantha Pryke (12)

All A Child Needs Is . . .

Every day a child is beaten,
Every day a child needs tlc,
Every day a child is used as a punchbag,
Every day a child needs a friend,
Every day a child is the victim of a bad temper,
Every day a child needs a mother's care,
Every day a child goes to sleep crying,
Every day a child needs emotional security.

All a child needs is . . . to be loved by you!

Jamie Rich (14)

FREEDOM

The day I was born my mamma cried,
I still see her tears as I was taken from her side.
Her screams as I left soon became mine,
As I saw my new home where I would spend time.
Shackled and whipped until I obeyed,
Every night I cried and I prayed.

Why can't I be free?
Like those who control me.
Walk down the streets with my head held high,
Walk down the streets and look the white man in the eye.

In my teenage years my anger grew,
For all the white man put me through.
I worked my days with little sleep,
My sweat, it poured, to earn my keep.
Through this all I met my wife,
We had a child and gave it life.

Why can't I be free?
Like those who control me.
Walk down the streets with my head held high,
Walk down the streets and look the white man in the eye.

As my years aged on I watched my son,
Seeing him too, ruled by the whip and the gun.
As I grew an old man I feared death was near,
Though I felt pain no more and never shed a tear.
And as I draw last breath . . . my eyes open wide,
My life at its end but I am happy inside.

For now I am free, no white man can trouble me.
Free from hurt, pain and hate, free to knock on Heaven's gate.
Where I know I can walk with my head held high,
Where I know I can look the
Lord in the eye.

Heather Stirling (15)

It's My Life!

I've just escaped six of the worst weeks of my life.
For those six weeks I spent in a wheelchair
with my left leg high in the air.

Most of my friends were really kind
and some a little too much, which made me feel kind of uncomfortable
and made me feel different in an unpleasant way.
Others joked, laughed, mocked and made me feel I'd done
something wrong.
Teachers gave me special treatment, and pushed me round the school,
which I was more than capable of doing.
Pushing myself round the school, people opened doors for me,
stepped aside for me, stared at me.
Others came from behind and started pushing me where I didn't want to
go, but there was nothing I could do about it.
People made me feel totally dependant but I tried to hold in my anger,
because I knew they were only trying to help and I know that if they
knew how I felt, they probably wouldn't have done it,
but they don't and they did.

Pushing round the town was a real job.
The pavement was never even.
Even pushing on one wheel, I still veered off, swerving left or right.
Being pushed around town, that was easier for me and definitely harder
for the other person but it made me feel vulnerable.
I couldn't see who was behind me, whether it was my mum, my dad, a
friend or a stranger.
Only the person pushing me could realise how difficult it was pushing
myself round town,
but the rest, that was still locked inside.
I felt ensnared, like I was cut off from the outside world,
like I was in prison, so deprived.
But now I'm out of my wheelchair, not walking very well,
but managing.

And now, I am closer to appreciating how hard it is for other men,
women, or even children who permanently need a wheelchair
and if I were in their position, I don't think I could cope.
But now, this is my life again, and everything is back to how it was.
Well, almost and I no longer feel ensnared, vulnerable, scared because
this is my life!

Christopher Hill (13)

THEME PARK

When you're feeling down
And nothing's going right
There's somewhere you can go
From morning until night.

It's like another world,
Where worries don't belong
Everyone is happy
And the air is full of song.

There's so much to do!
Something for everyone
And whizzing round on all the rides,
Is very, very, good fun.

Especially the roller coaster
With its winding, twisting track
It may seem scary
But once you're on, there's no turning back!

But sadly, there comes a time
When the end is near,
You have to go home,
But you can come back next year!

Hayley Irwin (15)

What It's Like To Be Me

Sometimes it's hard to be as old as I am,
Acting 'stress free' and cheerful is such a sham.
Being told I'm just a child, I know nothing of pain,
Then why do I feel such sorrow, grief and disdain?
I sometimes wonder why I feel this way,
Like I have no control over what I do or say,
Adults call it hormones or just a phrase,
Don't they remember, or is it lost in a haze?
I'd like to take them back when they were me,
Struggling to keep control as if lost at sea.
Then maybe they'd understand and change how they act.
But we can't blame them, it's just a fact!
When you get old you can hardly remember
What it feels like to have your emotions in a blender!
Which is why now, I am writing this all,
So if I ever have children I can recall,
That these years are not full of childhood glee
And I will always know what it's like to be me.

Cali Madincea (14)

Untitled

Life is really fun,
It feels bright like the sun,
As I get older I feel I have power
Like a hot jet shower.

Life will be getting harder in the long term
But it is important to keep firm.
Exams get near
We start to fear.

We will make new friends,
Who's your friend it all depends,
Your friend will make you or break you,
So look after them and yourself too!

Pranav Bhanot (14)

All Alone, By Myself

Here I sit, all alone in my corner,
Nobody to love, no one who cares,
Pondering about my troubles and woes,
Just all alone, no one but myself.

I walk along the path of life,
No one in sight, like a barren desert,
Streets deserted, houses empty,
I'm all alone, no one but myself.

I run a marathon from north to south,
Passing silent cities and dark towns,
Not a bark or shout to be heard,
Only my footsteps, all alone by myself.

I enter a cafe with music playing,
No waiter or customer in sight,
All I ask is companionship and someone to talk,
But here I am all alone, by myself.

I glimpse a picture of two people in love,
Wondering where my friends have gone,
So here I sit alone in my corner,
Just all alone, no one but myself.

Neal Shakespeare-Walker (15)

The Summer

The school bell rings,
Every teenager speeds out of control through the doors,
The stampede, the chaos and the adrenaline rush,
To think this is all because of what summer brings.

We all go out to parties, raves and discos,
Where the boys shout, 'Would you be my girlfriend?'
And the girls have a dilemma about it being hot in here,
But we never forget Thong Song from Sisqo.

Girls and boys are going on dates,
The girls are looking fly,
The boys are looking hot,
But we always have time for our mates.

We have water fights and grass fights,
We go out for shopping,
We splash at swimming,
Watch videos with your mates all night.

Also spending time with family is great,
Going to the cinema,
Eating out together,
Even watching TV together till late.

Now the summer is ending we never
Forget the special days and nights,
The special days with our friends and family,
The days that were so full of adrenaline we'd never forget,
So when the summer comes, make sure it's the best,
Because as teenagers it's our given right.

Daisy Daniels (15)

My World

Hi! My name is Gemma,
I have brown eyes and brown hair,
I am fourteen and love to draw,
I also like visiting the fair.
I live with my parents and Georgia,
I do not argue with Mum nor Dad,
Having mood swings with my sister,
But I suppose it's not all that bad.

I have a group of real cool friends,
We hang out in the park,
Football and chatting is our thing,
We stroll home when it gets dark.
Telling each other our problems,
Which is sometimes about boys we like,
Complaining about looks and fashion,
Such as Elle, Gucci and Nike.

I love to listen to music,
My favourite band is Blue,
I enjoy going to parties,
I also like Backstreet Boys too.
I find that in my room, I can relax,
Get away from the stresses of life,
Emotions spinning around in my head,
Causing me confusion and strife.

I dream to be a fashion designer,
Interior design will do,
Leave school and go to college,
Maybe university too.

Gemma Blake (14)

Read Me!

I have struggled
To write a poem
To keep you all going and going.

Oh I do wish
You will read
My poem that I so need

To be the best
You can buy
Or you see
I might just cry.

Poetry is the best thing
Pen and paper could ever bring

It helps me to express what I think
Or my paper may be as blank as a kitchen sink.

I am at the end of my fantastic poem,
I hope it did keep you going and going.

Vincenza Stevens (13)

No Will To Cry

A cutting blade to make an open wound,
Trying to bleed the pain away,
Adrenaline riding round my body,
Giving me an intense emotional high,
Thinking, can I go deeper or will I die?
Long-sleeved jumpers, I must wear to lie,
For just a while I feel just fine,
No pain, no hatred,
No will to cry.

Gillian Henderson (15)

KID!

When you're a kid,
And very, very small,
Everyone else looks incredibly tall,
When you are big in height,
You wish you were small,
Then life starts to feel you're under no rule.
And when you grow older,
Everyone is mean,
It's a really hard life being a teen,
But when you are young,
What will be your ultimate fate?
What will become
Of that little kid
That everyone knew?
To be kind and friendly and helpful to you,
But now who's the rebel?
Voice from soprano to treble
And after all that has happened,
You start to look back at the good and the bad,
The stuff that always made you mad
And you say: I wish I were a kid!

Nicholas Jones (14)

THE JUNGLE BEACH

Crabs snigger at the whimpering fish,
Sand scurries away from the cliffs,
Pebbles scream from the crushing rock,
They make a barrier like a canal lock,
Hermits titter away from the motion,
From out there is the smirking killing ocean.

Jessica Butcher (13)

MY DAD'S EYEBROW

My dad's eyebrow,
Like one big creature,
The most hideous type of facial feature.

My dad's eyebrow,
Never-ending,
Always straight and never bending.

My dad's eyebrow,
Across his face,
Stretching up and into space.

My dad's eyebrow,
Big and thick,
You couldn't beat it with a stick.

My dad's eyebrow,
Just like him,
Long and big and very thin.

James Kaufmann (13)

A TRAIN JOURNEY

A journey is a train,
That speeds like a bullet,
Under and over bridges,
In many dark tunnels.

A journey is a train,
It's like a river,
In and out of stations,
Just like the wind.

A journey is a train,
It sticks to a track like a runner,
Round all the corners,
Sprinting along the track.

Sarah Worrall (13)

LIFE

We are the thorns
Entwined in the rose bush that is life
The marks which we leave can
Stain with peace or with strife
With each year that passes
A precious petal falls
And the rose becomes bare
When life no longer calls.
The secrets within us still lie
And guilt can wave for eternity
Just as the poison ivy
Wraps around the living tree.
The tears which we cry
Form pools of emptiness
Therefore embrace
The warm feeling of forgiveness.
In every fresh whisper
Our passion still lives on
You leave me with your presence
Even when you're gone
Life is fragile, though
It has no meaning
It is up to you and you alone
To make it mean something.

Amy Crossman (15)

TEENAGE LIFE

I woke up this morning knowing it would be the first day of school,
A day in which the teachers can rule.
I was on my way to catch the dreaded school bus,
Where all the new kids will be making a fuss.
Invitations were handed out by a popular boy in my class,
Who said this party will be his last.
I was excited that I was chosen to go, but I knew my
Mum and dad would say no.
The hours dragged on, but soon everyone was gone.
My friends came over, just as my mum pulled up in our old Rover.
I took my friends to my house and showed them my
Sister's little brown mouse,
The next place I took my friends was my bedroom,
Which Mum said looked like a tomb.
I showed my friends all my cool stuff,
Then Mum burst in complaining about all the fluff.
My friends soon went home and that was when I was left alone,
I went to talk about the party to Mum and Dad,
But straight after Mum and Dad checked I was in bed,
I crept out the window and fell on my dog Ned,
He barked all night long, as I was told I was in the wrong,
Mum and Dad said that I'm not allowed out for a long time,
That's when I felt I had committed a crime.
It's hard being someone my age,
You feel like you're trapped in a cage.

Sarah Finn (15)

THE RACE

Nerves tense up as you await your race,
Try to keep up with that fast running pace.
Throughout the race your heart is throbbing,
I hope at the end you won't be sobbing!

Almost there, the finishing line is near,
Keep pushing harder, banish that fear.
For the goal is in sight, the race almost done,
Yes, it's over, hooray, the race has been won!

Zara Smith (13)

INTERPRETATION OF LIFE

Origination.
Imagining, creating and fabricating.
The threads of being are entwined.
Our most prominent feature,
Is truly the mind.

Contemplation.
Thinking, wondering and searching.
Is something we all do,
In the mind and in the heart,
Searching for what is true.

Adaptation.
Changing, questioning and perplexing,
Is the game of destiny.
Innocence of a child expelled,
And replaced with maturity.

Aspiration.
Dreaming, expressing and idealising,
In what we hope to achieve,
The elements of elevation,
Is our dreams we can weave.

Satisfaction by greatness,
Derived from a star.
Humbled by the soul.
We are what we are.

Raunak Singh (15)

Is She Alive? Is She Dead?

I stand, unable to move for the shock of what has happened
I watch the many people digging in the rubble of what was my house
Yet I cannot move to help
Fear has set in and fixed me to the spot.

Is she alive? Is she dead?
These questions keep turning over and over in my head
Like a great whirlwind clouding up my mind
The answers to these, I have to find.

A chill shoots up my spine, as I pull a blanket around my shoulders
Yet it is cold I do not feel it, for I am numb with anticipation and fear
And still I cannot find the strength to help
Terror has set in and drained away my energy.

Is she dead? Is she alive?
These questions keep turning over and over in my mind
Like a great storm brewing overhead
The prayers for these answers must be said.

As I look on, a cry is heard among those searching the rubble.
Suddenly, my heart misses a beat - could it be? Is she there . . . alive?
Feeling returns to my body, and my mind is cleared for one brief moment.
As I rush over to where they stand
Expectation sets in and gives me hope.

Is she alive? Is she dead?
These thoughts continue to clog my head
The fog has lifted slightly in my mind
My daughter, I am closer to find.

I kneel down and place my ear to a small gap in the rubble . . . silence
I listen again, straining with what strength I have regained . . .
A faint cry can be heard.
A cry of desperation . . . a cry of a frightened child . . .
The cry of my daughter.

She isn't dead. She is alive!
Sheer bliss and happiness fill my mind!
Those thoughts of darkness leave my head
Ecstasy and elation take over now instead.
More rubble is now cleared away
I now see my daughter, clear as day.
I lift her up, and hold her in my arms
She's now safe and free from harm.
Her small, pale face looks up into mine
From now on, I know everything will be fine.

Alice Morgan (14)

A 2002 TEEN!

When I was young, school was cool,
I had a friend for every finger and thumb,
But when I look now, there's only one pal,
Who's just as good as they come.

The geeks of the class don't have Adidas,
All they have is science and maths.

I'm sick of the pressure,
It's too much to take,
You have to be popular and
Brainy for god's sake.

When I get older, I want a good job,
My mum always says it's harder these days.

So I'll stay in and study,
Hope not to worry,
Maybe one day I'll have lots of money!

Michelle Hodgson (14)

MORNINGS

The sun peeps through my window and I get this awful thought,
A sneaky feeling lurks in me telling me to get out of bed I ought,
I can hear loud voices booming up through my bedroom floor,
I really don't want to go to school today,
Of days off there should be more.

I clamber into my uniform, it's a hideous colour blue,
Mum's vocal chords are calling me, oh I can't wait
until the day is through.
My eyes are sore and sleepy and the kitchen looks so bright,
I eat my breakfast lazily and then Mum says, 'See you tonight.'
The whole school day's ahead of me, ain't that a gloomy thought,
Oh I haven't finished my algebra, I hope I don't get caught,
I look inside my lunch box, hoping that will cheer me up,
I stare in disbelief, as all Mum's packed is a cup.

Elizabeth Williams (13)

GROWING PAINS

Growing up can be a bore
And sometimes seems just like a chore,
It all seems easy when we're young
And feel content when sucking a thumb.
We have no knowledge of murder or rape
And never need time to just escape,
We have no pressures from family and friends,
But when we hit ten that bliss ends,
Growing up can be a bore
And often feels just like a chore!

Jennie Mawson (13)

Teenage Blues

Brothers, sisters, mums and dads, they're all the same you know,
'Do this, do that!' and 'Blah! Blah! Blah!' That's all they seem to go!
I'm always doing chores for my parents, boring ones like
washing the pots,
They always make me do them though I hate them lots and lots.
At school you can't get away from it all, it's just the same with
teachers,
You can't mess around to do anything stupid cos they stick to
you like leeches!
I'm always arguing with my brother, it always ends up in a fight,
He puts me under so much stress that haunts my sleep at night!
My mum and dad aren't quite so bad, they just don't understand,
But they're always there (well nearly) if I need a helping hand.
My mates sometimes don't listen and just don't seem to care,
But that's OK cos I've got others and I'll take my problems elsewhere.
It's sometimes better to be on my own and have a bit of peace,
It's ever so calm and tranquil that the stress and troubles cease.

Carmilla Hague (13)

Butterflies

I looked up, into the blue sky
And saw the most beautiful butterflies,
Flying up high, with no troubles to
Make them laugh or cry,
I think butterflies are wonderful creatures,
They also have brilliant features,
Like their vivid wings which make them fly,
Butterflies, butterflies all around,
Pretty and colourful, they are born to not make a sound.

Hayley Diehl (13)

TEACHER

Vulture leering over books,
Children watching in case she looks
And sees that Jenny has no pen
And Tom is now sat next to Ben,
That Tracey's passing notes along,
To check if her answer's right or wrong
And also if Rosie fancies Jack
And, 'Do you like my new rucksack?'
    'Becky stop being a pest!
    Concentrate and do your test,
    For if I find you get no marks,
    I'll send you off to Mr Parks,
    He'll teach you a lesson, yes he will,
    You'll be so scared, you'll sit straight still
    And if he has to phone your mum,
    You'll get a smack upon your bum!
    So now get on and do your work,
    Don't think with me that you can shirk.
    Pick up your pen and show you're able,
    So we can be top of the school league table!'

Helen Scholey (13)

TWO BLIND MEN

The human eye sees a lot,
But the blind eye always sees more.

An open eye may see the world,
But a blind eye can feel a lot more.

The image of an open eye can see from dawn to dusk,
But the image of a blind man goes from Heaven to Earth.

And from the hells of Heaven,
To the heavens of Hell.

An open man may ask how you are,
But only a blind man may know your answer.

Molly Huq (14)

The Formula 1 Race

The cars line up behind the light,
The Monaco track is quite a fright.
The lights go out, the engines roar,
The noise enhances, more and more.
They race to the U-turn, over the hill,
Their speed is increasing, oh what a thrill!
The chicane's just ahead, they slam on the brakes,
Michael's in front but Ralph overtakes.
They zoom into the tunnel, who's in the lead?
Their position's important for the points that they need.
They emerge, what a shock, Ralph's down in fourth,
They round a chicane and head for the north.
The tension is mounting, they're nearing the grid,
But there's oil on the track and Button just slid.
Ralph's back in second, Michael is first,
But Button's now twentieth, this race is his worst.
He's entered the pits and he's damaged his car,
If it doesn't get fixed, he'll not get far.
They're over the line and Michael has won,
He'll go round again for his victory run.
The corks pop off the bottles, there's champagne in the air,
It is rather a waste but does anyone care?

Martin Piper (13)

The First World War

The first World War began in 1914,
I was taken away by men who were mean.

The trenches were filthy, they were made out of mud,
There were diseases amongst us and many covered in blood.

When we were not fighting, we wrote to our friends,
It was often heartbreaking, we hoped it would end.

I remember one time, when a good friend died,
It was very upsetting, everyone cried.

One night we were woken, from a blast of a gun,
We retaliated for hours, until the sun shone.

It went all quiet, I had blood dripping from my head,
We crawled out of our trenches, where we roamed the dead.

The war is over, we finally won,
I can't wait to get home, where there's peace and no guns.

I had fought for my country, I had many moans,
But there's nothing better than being back home.

Charlene Griffiths (14)

Friends

Friends are the people I trust and care for,
Friends are the people who encourage you,
Friends are people you go to parties with,
Friends are people you go shopping with,
Friends are those people who care for you,
Friends are those people who trust you too,
Friends can be anyone you talk to.

Naomi Crewe (14)

RESPECTING STREET CRED

Street cred seems to me
To be
A form of respect.
Yet not formed on the basis
Of who you are,
Or your beliefs and character.
But formed on what you wear,
Where you hang out -
The 'tribe' you belong to.

We've all been there,
Where are hasty actions
Determine our cred:

In front of a crowd,
That geeky girl from
Next door
Attempts to start a conversation.
With you.

Street cred visibly draining, diminishing.

A distant voice
Resonating in your mind,
Replies cuttingly.

Street cred swells,
Respect rises.

The geek turns aside.
The glint of hurt
Half-hidden underneath
Her eyelids.

Killing others' own respect.
Just to earn some street cred,
Just for a little respect.

Laura Wills (14)

SMOKING

Smoking is bad
And makes people sad,
It makes you unwell
And also makes you smell.

Teenagers think it's cool
But they're acting like a fool,
It makes them addicted
Just what people predicted.

Smokers think they're tough
And act really rough,
They make others get hurt
And throw them in the dirt.

I'm never gonna smoke
Cos it's not a joke,
So don't go smoking fags
Or turn into a heap of rags!

Tasleema Quayyum (13)

WAR

People die every day
So why do we have to pay?
Without even getting our say
War is wrong,
We've got to stay strong.

Families are killed or torn apart,
So why don't they have a heart,
War is wrong,
We've got to stay strong.

Important people say it's right,
But we know it's wrong to fight,
War is wrong,
We've got to stay strong,
We've got to stay strong.

Nicola Bradshaw (13)

A Disordered World

Teenage girls have a hard time,
From school and parents and friends,
But life gets real tough,
And you think you can cope!
So don't cry, don't cut, don't be sick!

It may help for the moment,
But the pain eventually shows
And the scars take a long time to heal,
So stop for a moment and think it through slowly,
Just stop, take a minute, be free!
So don't cry, don't cut, don't be sick!

If you listen to others,
Block it all out,
You're not fat,
Don't lose weight,
Don't be stupid,
They're immature and don't understand,
How you feel deep inside, oh so pressured!
So don't cry, don't cut, don't be sick!

Just be free,
Live your life
And enjoy what you have
Because today we live in a disordered world!

Amy White (14)

What Is Green?

What is green?
For a start it's a colour
And the scary Martian's
Hopefully not your mother.

A hat to wear,
An apple or pear,
A punk's hair.

Lemmings and flower stems
And sometimes you'll find emerald gems.

The funkiest colour to be seen
Is green
And grasshoppers are green,
When they jump and hop and shimmer and gleam.

Green is the colour of ecology, cleanliness,
But clean is not green.
It is not what it looks like,
Not what it may seem.

Green is sewerage,
The colour of a scream
And the leaves on the beanstalk
In your nightmare of a dream.

Green is the sound,
Of zombies walking,
Green is a gang of
Criminals stalking.

Green is the sporty new
Mini Cooper,
100 miles per hour through town,
Now that's what I call super!

You can smell green
In an empty alleyway,
The fluorescent graffiti on the walls,
Or in the unlit subway.

Arvin Feltham (13)

MY FEELINGS

As I started year 9
I was very excited
I could pick my subjects
That I wanted for the next 2 years
But the bad thing is SATs,
Every teenager has to go through this!
My emotions were everywhere
First I didn't care, just another test but as the time came
I started to worry,
Sitting in the hall thinking what was I going to do?
I started to panic, then my mind went blank,
But then I told myself I could this and get the grade I needed,
After terrible SATs had finished,
We had to put our option into the head of the year,
PE, food technology, sociology, maths, English, science and French,
That's what I wanted.
A couple of weeks later, the head of the year told me that I
Couldn't do sociology.
As I felt the tears one by one strolling down my face,
I got up to go and I felt terrible,
I rang my mum,
My mum being my mum, she sorted it out for me
And I was allowed to do sociology,
During this time, I felt heartbroken, as I really wanted to do this subject
And now it is the holidays and my feelings are,
Well what do you think, it is the holidays!

Lisa Rogers (14)

My Perspective Of Life

I believe in destiny,
For all that it brings
And I believe integrity,
Is a virtue for all things.

I believe humanity,
Does not live in vain
And I believe in compassion,
Yet I am not insane.

I view another dimension,
As not such an insipid dream
And I believe our existence,
Is more than it may seem.

I believe malevolence,
Is the worst force of emotion
And I believe a mother,
Should have enduring devotion.

I view an act of betrayal,
As incredibly hard to forgive,
But I believe it is important,
For times we encounter as we live.

I understand why society,
Can often follow the crowd,
But I view individuality,
As something of which to be proud.

I believe that our existence,
Is a gift that should be treasured
And I believe that we should enjoy it,
For happiness should not be measured.

Amanda Chappell (14)

TEEN SPECIES

We're all at the age now
Where we should all know how,
To tie our own shoelaces
And pack our own suitcases
And be responsible in things that we do.

When in school
You shouldn't act cruel,
To teachers who think they know best
And take that god damn history test,
It's much better than looking a fool.

When at home,
Don't sit about and moan,
But don't go out alone
Because you might not make it back home,
These things should be taken into account.

When doing homework,
Make sure it's your own work
And take time and consideration in what you do
And teachers may feel merit is due,
So don't copy, that's one thing you should never do.

So take into account your learning
And make sure your eyesight and hearing's intact,
Because you need that for a fact
And take pride in everything you do.

We're all at the age now,
Where we should all know how,
To tie our own shoelaces
And pack our own suitcases
And be responsible in things that we do.

Emma Walker (13)

A TEENAGE STAGE

Fatigued, like a worn out piece of cloth,
Drained like a pressed flower,
I slide lazily under the duvets,
Feeling like milk gone sour.

I'm withered like an old leaf,
Feel like a plate of mushy peas,
The room is still its boring self
And hours feel like weeks.

I'm as worthless as a battered can
And just want to be left alone,
I'm as wasted as a worn out shoe
And don't want to get up to the phone.

I'm as sluggish as the snails in the garden
And as tired as the end of the day,
Everything seems so boring and worthless,
I want the world to just go away.

I'm lethargic, lifeless, listless and lazy,
I'm a seedy and slushy slime,
I'm dull, drowsy, torpid and tired
And unnoticeably slipping through time.

I'm a teenager just feeling worthless
I'm at a Mondayish kind of age.
I shouldn't worry if I don't seem myself
Because it's just a passing stage!

Kate Moore (14)

THE PERFECT PLACE

A place without tears,
A place without pain,
A place where war and conflict
Has not left its bloody stain.

A place without division,
A place not shadowed in the dark,
A place where separation,
Has not struck and left its mark.

A place without variance,
Untarnished by dissension,
A place without strife
Made hungry from contention.

A place where joy and smiling
Can be seen dancing in the rain,
A place where proposals of peacefulness,
Are not rendered and broken in vain.

A place built on unity,
From agreement and accord,
A placed raised by coalition,
By harmony and concord.

A place where we are unified,
Joined by love and care,
I'm sure a place like this exists,
But the question is, where?

Amy Nelson (15)

Love

Your love is like a red, red rose,
It runs through my veins from my head to my toes,
When you hold me, my pulse begins to race,
Now that you're gone, I can't wait to see your face.

Since I met you long ago,
I've walked back, to and fro,
Looking for my long-lost love,
An angel sent from high above.

When I see your face again,
I'll walk through hail or sleet or rain,
I'll do whatever you want me to,
All I want is to be with you.

Now we're back together,
I want it to last forever,
No matter what it takes,
We'll make it through,
All I want is to be with you.

Rebecca Hale (14)

Family

F riendly,
A ctive,
M emorable,
I mportant,
L ovable,
Y es, this is my family.

Shahzana Begum (13)

AFGHANISTAN

Afghanistan
Country of many troubled with strife,
Its people permanently fight for life.

Drought and famine takes its toll,
Enough to drain one's soul.

People of Afghanistan, not a care for war,
They say not any more.

Bombs reign in,
Seeking one enemy,
Run, run people of Afghanistan
Seeking one enemy.

Bombs may cease,
Temporary peace,
When oh when will war cease?

Hailey Cook (15)

GREAT NAN

G reat nan's coming to stay,
R eady to come on her way,
E veryone is happy
A nd great nan is excited too,
T elling everyone about her move.

N an is looking forward to it
A nd I am counting the days,
N an will be on her way soon and
everyone will cheer hooray!

Emma Webb (14)

EMMA

Emma is my sister's name,
She is two years old,
She likes to play a little game,
Come find me I was told.

Emma likes to dance and sing,
She likes to watch the telly,
She loves to wear her golden ring,
And stash things in dad's welly.

Emma she has light blonde hair,
She also has brown eyes,
She likes to show me lots of care,
And hardly ever cries.

I'm so glad that she's my sister,
She's so cute and cool,
If she left I'd surely miss her,
She definitely does rule!

Cheryl Read (14)

WHAT IS CARING?

What is caring?
Who knows what it is,
Could it be when you love someone,
Or when you don't.

I care for my family,
My friends too,
But I don't understand,
What should I do?

It could be a feeling when you're
Friend is sick,
Or a feeling for someone you
Walk by on the street,
Who knows what it is,
What is caring?

Cheryl Fuller (15)

DEPRESSED

To me the day is cold and blue,
To others gold and warm,
They run about with happy smiles,
They do not feel my storm.

I could write a thousand books,
Or write a million lines,
I've tried to cry, but tears won't come,
Can't say what's in my mind.

And still I walk, head high above,
My body slumped and slow,
I smile with all the others now,
Nothing seems to show.

I don't know why I feel like this,
I don't know why I hide,
Emotions running past my lips,
Everything's inside.

The world just seems to be a blur,
The sky is always grey,
I pass grey fields, grey hills, grey cars,
Another happy day.

Nicole Willis (13)

Teenage Life

The dark cloud is coming
Teenage life has come
Fast food and late TV
The dark cloud is coming
School sucks and my bed rocks
It's a teenage life
Hardcore music and killer movies
It's a teenage life
Girls are my life
My world has turned upside down
It's a teenage life
My computer is the best
My room is in a mess
It's a teenage life
There will be a time
When it will pass but
Teenage life is the best.

Ged Paton (15)

Colours Of The Earth

Red as a rose which has just bloomed,
Orange as a setting sun in the distance,
Yellow as a melon ready to eat,
Green as fresh grass which has just been cut,
Blue as the sea which you play in,
Pink as candyfloss ready to eat
Purple as a violet which has just been planted,
White as snow which has just fallen,
Brown as mud which is freshly dug,
Black as coal which is burning.

Kirsty Griffiths (15)

Boys!

You find a guy
Who caught your eye
He made you sigh
And almost cry.
He took your heart
At the very start
And by the end, tore it apart.
You thought at first he was the guy
To hold you close and feel alright.
Soon you saw this was all a lie
And thought you would just rather die.
This is how some girls feel
But some don't think it's such a deal,
It gets us down when they treat us like toys,
What are we talking about?
We're talking about boys!

Kirsty Nicholls (14)

Teenage Girls!

Make-up, spots, clothes and boys,
Are the things we've replaced for toys!
Trendy, townie, diva or tarty,
Whichever you are, you enjoy a party!
Boob tubes and skirts, trousers and tops,
A girly night out or Top of the Pops,
Chocolate, chips, cake or curry,
Things to avoid if you don't wanna tummy!
Parents are out, you're home alone,
Nail extensions complete, non-acetone.
So slap on the make-up, pull on the gear,
Get ready to party, the crowd are all here!

Laura Smyth (13)

FEELINGS

When I feel sad, I mope around,
When I feel happy, I jump and shout,
When I'm embarrassed, I curl up inside,
I feel like a knot with a million butterflies.
When I'm angry, I stomp and moan,
When I'm in love, I write a poem.
When I'm tired, I yawn and squirm,
It's like I'm a flower ready to bloom.
When I'm excited, I jump and shout,
No one can help me out of my rant.
If you have no feelings then you're as cold as ice,
But if you're like me,
Then you're bursting with life.

Deborah Wells (13)

A SLEEPLESS NIGHT

A long, cold winter's night,
I lay in my bed with an awful fright,
The wind whistled through a gap under my door,
I heard creaky noises from under the floor,
Trees tumbled, twisted shadows on my wall,
I heard a faint distant echo call,
A knock I heard, a flap of a bird,
A definite scream, a shining beam,
The rain poured down, splashed on the ground,
Lightning struck and thunder made a rumbling sound,
I shivered and turned, worried and hid,
I don't know, maybe I'm being a stupid kid!

Hannah Robinson (14)

THE LAST OBSESSION

The last obsession was an old one
The obsessions were never rare
Because she was always hungry
The obsessions were always there.

What do you buy the chameleon
Disguised as a girl?
What do you buy the teen
With their own dreamworld?

She was like a yo-yo
Her mind could change any day
One week she loved something
The next, she'd run the other way.

The last obsession was an old one
The obsessions were never rare
They came and went so often
They made her peers despair.

How can you possibly keep up
With an ever-changing mind?
How do you tame a brain so hyper?
A lone train of thought is hard to find.

What do you do to help
When a person can't think straight?
What do you do to distract them
Before it's much too late?

The last obsession was an old one
The obsessions were never rare
But one day they went away -
Suddenly the real world was there.

Clare Stone (15)

THE TEENAGER'S WORLD

What I'm feeling deep inside,
I've never felt before,
There's a *burning* in my heart,
And in my very soul.

The *pressure* is too much,
How can I cope?
I need some encouragement,
Some love and some hope.

Can't think about my future,
My dreams or my *fears*
It hurts too much,
Don't want to push the tears.

My head is banging,
Blood rushing through my veins,
I need time alone,
Don't want to go *insane.*

My feelings are tangled,
My *emotions* run wild,
Don't you understand?
I'm no longer a child!

Anneka Sawhney

UNTITLED

One day I'm really sad,
The next, I'm very mad,
Sometimes I'm very grumpy,
Oh my life is very bumpy.

I'm angry at my parents,
I'm angry at my friends,
I don't know what I'm doing,
I want it to go away.

Ross Taylor (13)

A Roller Coaster

Hey, hey, hey!
Come on everybody, come on,
Roll, roll and roll, on a roller coaster.
Glide on the Gigantic Bomber,
Roll, roll and roll, on a roller coaster.
The queue is long and wide,
Enjoy every minute of the ride,
Roll, roll and roll, on a roller coaster.
With electric currents,
High and low,
Round and round it goes,
Roll, roll and roll, on a roller coaster.
The sound is loud and harsh,
Bangs the rider with a bash,
Roll, roll and roll, on a roller coaster.
A freak expression storms on the rider's face,
The horror of being in such a place,
Roll, roll and roll, on a roller coaster.
Screams, fear and a yell,
All make life a hell,
Roll, roll and roll, on a roller coaster.
Lose your mentality for a while,
Show a brave face as inside you die.
Come on everybody, come on,
Roll, roll and roll on a roller coaster.

Nabiha Iqbal (14)

WHO'S MY BEST FRIEND?

First thing in the morning,
In the day, or late at night.
I never give pre-warning,
Just any time's alright.

He's always there, my mate; my chum,
Ever ready to make me laugh,
I've never seen him glum,
You'll probably think I'm daft.

He helps me with my homework,
My charts and graphs and that.
I've never seen him want to shirk,
Or asks for anything back.

He helps me to communicate,
With friends both near and far,
And keeps my shopping up-to-date,
I don't even need a car.

I might as well describe him,
The source of all my joy,
This darling saint without a sin,
And no it's not a boy.

He's a bubbly purple-coloured ape,
Who lives in my PC
Now . . . I see you start to gape,
Bonzi, of course, who else can it be?

Martina Macdonald (14)

Wonder

Patience, trust - two things that
    should get me through.
Instead impatience, cheating are
    getting me through.
Struggling day after day,
    it gets worse.
Cruel, that is all it is, for
    I have a lot of hunger in me.
To perform, use my talent and fight
    against the world.
But that is all just a dream,
    not a reality.
My greatest virtue, is the fire, the
    blaze, I have inside me
Which is pure terror, as it
    gets worse day by day.
Moving, burning through me,
    till hatred has consumed my patience.
Depth of blaze, leaves me felt
    as if I have been used.
I feel like a freak, day and night
    are pure terror and horror.
And I feel like all my dreams
    have been taken.
Which just leaves me to
    wonder . . .

Taybah Fiaz (13)

Love Is . . .

Love is . . .
The bubbly feeling you compete with inside
And the prickly things running up your spine.
Like a firework exploding!

You are lost without each other,
Together you are complete as one,
Nothing else matters at all
And no one else can make you fall.
You can't hide it,
You can't destroy it,
It is always there,
As you're every thought
And every breath,
Staring you in the face,
Like the beating of my heart!

Love is . . .
A warm summer's day
And a rush of emotions running wild,
Like the beauty of a red rose!

Fern Bagley (14)

I Hate School

I hate school,
But other people think it's cool,
Teachers like to moan
And groan.
But when it is lunch,
They start to crunch,
Instead of moaning
And groaning!

One of my teachers thinks he's so cool,
Because he drives his fast cars to school.
He tries to make people laugh,
But it makes him look like a giraffe.
He comes back from holiday really brown,
As his name is Mr Brown!

Sarah Bliss (14)

WHAT I FEEL!

When I feel love, I always give a cheerful smile,
The energy it gives me could make me run a mile.
The feeling brings inspiration straight to you,
Through the clouds, out of the blue.

When I fill with sadness, I also fill with rage,
Which makes; me want to lock my problems up in a cage.
I'd study them for hours, to discover what makes them tick,
Even though I know it would definitely make me feel sick.

When I feel guilty about lying to a loyal friend,
I begin to wish I'd told the truth and it drives me round the bend.
Because when you have a friendship you don't want to break,
There are always certain risks you must be willing to take.

I am like an onion, I have many different layers in my life.
And it is these feelings which tend to give me all my strife.

Being a teenager is harder than you know.
Give us some space and allow us to grow.
As adulthood approaches, we will begin to understand,
How to bring our heads out from beneath the sand.

The modern gizmos and gadgets, we take for granted too much,
I wonder how we'd feel if they were taken out of our clutch . . .

Rachel Wyncoll (13)

The Mind Of A Teenager

The mind of a teen
Doesn't often get seen
But we all have to be one
Even your mum!

Being a teenager like me
People don't like to see
Us as we are.

Whether you like school
It's up to you
People worry about it being uncool.

Magazines tell us how we should look
But hey, it's only a book!
Many of us have dreams
But sometimes they aren't what they seem!

The mind of a teen
Doesn't often get seen
But we all have to be one
Even your mum!

Natasha Cook (14)

Myself And Feelings

Sometimes I am happy,
I sing and laugh.

Sometimes I'm sad,
I cry and hide.

Sometimes I'm mad,
I scream and shout.

Sometimes I'm confused,
I don't know what to do.

But don't ask me I'm just a
Teenager like you.

Lisa Norman (14)

I Hate The Way . . .

I hate the way you talk about me
And the fact you always stare,
I hate the way you drive me crazy
And when you never seem to care.

I hate the way you make me feel
And the fact we always fight,
I hate it when you're clever,
I hate it when you're right.

I hate it when you tease me
And the fact you play mind games.
I hate it when you annoy me
And sometimes call me names.

I hate the fact you're so tall
And I hate it when you lie,
I hate it when you make me laugh,
Even more, when you make me cry.

I hate it when you're not around
And the fact that you don't call,
But most of all, I hate the way
I don't hate you at all.

Jacklyn Connelly (15)

My Family!

My family,
There's six of us in all,
Occasionally seven,
There's my dad he drives us all mad,
What with all that moaning and groaning,
But then I pity the poor bugger, after all he is married to my mother!

That brings me on to my mother,
Now I do love her
And most of the time she's OK,
But occasionally she may get a bit moody,
We daren't mention,
But we know it's pre-menstrual tension,
But then again being married to my dad,
Well that's enough to drive anyone mad!

Then there's my big sister,
She spends half her life wasted
And that gets Dad well frustrated!

Then there's my twin,
She's smart and she's sensible
And the way she behaves is never unmentionable!

Then there's me,
Well where to begin,
I'm your typical teenager,
Maybe a little stranger!

Then there's my little sister,
She's kind, she's sweet,
Everyone says she's the nicest girl you could meet,
But I know otherwise,
You see she has a habit to antagonise!

Oh and the seventh person
Anyone aged 0-3 who needs a temporary family!

Alexandra Uttley (14)
(A member of a family that fosters)

UNTITLED

It's Wednesday morning, the day of your birthday,
You're now fifteen,
You walk downstairs to open your gifts,
The gift you've been waiting for isn't there.
You don't worry about it, maybe he has a good reason,
Your boyfriend hasn't sent you your gift,
You go off to school thinking it will turn up later,
The day goes on and the bell rings,
After three hours of being at home,
No phone calls, no gift, not even a card,
He didn't even apologise,
One of the closest people to you,
Forgot your birthday!

Stephanie Coles (15)

ANGER

Anger is a dragon that sleeps inside me,
It turns the sky to black, yet stabs you in the back,
But now is waiting, waiting.

Once awoken, grows intense and is extremely powerful,
The dragon comes,
He swells up inside me, trying to chance an outburst,
But now is waiting, waiting.

Red lights tickle and seduce walls of my delicate mind
And he licks them with icy fire:
Flickering, fearsome fire leaps up inside my clouded brain,
fogged by darkness
And they dance in my eyes,
But now he is waiting, waiting.

He wills me to set him free; but I resist the temptation,
For him to wreak havoc on my small, but already chaotic world,
His glow and his immense power keeps intensifying,
He is getting stronger,
For me harder;
Harder to keep control,
But now he is waiting, waiting.

He takes flight!
Trying desperately to uncover the door;
The door to a long awaited, but dreaded freedom.
But it is too well hidden
And escapes his red, penetrating, searching eye.

His own dragon forces him to burn and scorn the walls of his prison,
Even with his fiercest flames, he cannot escape the fortress
that holds him.

For now, at least, I can contain him,
But still he lies there,
Waiting,
Waiting . . .

Natalie Harding (14)

THE GIRL OF ALL SEASONS

The girl of all seasons is every man's dream,
She complements each season in the way girls do in dreams.

Her hair is long and silky,
It floats in the autumn breeze, like the autumn leaves falling from the trees.

Her teeth are clean and white,
They sparkle in the light,
Just like the first snow on a cold winter's night.

She always likes to be jolly, living an active life,
She doesn't know how to sit down, she's always full of life,
She could easily be mistaken for spring's new life.

She's the most intelligent girl I've ever seen,
She always looks forward, never where she's been,
She's brighter than the summer's sun and what more need I say.

There's only one girl this could be and for me it's Amy,
Everyone's got their own girl for all seasons
And all I can say is don't let her get away!

Wesley Savage (15)

The Summer Holidays

It is so much fun to be away from school,
But if you think the fun lasts, then you're a total fool.
It starts out *great* with loads of laughs,
But after a while it becomes hard graft.

You watch the TV and just generally chill out,
But there is always nagging parents about.
It's always, 'Do this, do that, sit up straight!
Go clean out your hamster and no it won't wait!'

And then there's your friends, or at least they say they are,
Some will meet up, some say it's too far.
So the holidays aren't really that much fun,
I suppose you could tidy the house to help out your mum.

It is so much fun to be away from school,
But if you think the fun lasts, then you're a total fool.
It starts out *great* with loads of laughs,
But after a while it becomes hard graft.

Kerry Becker (14)

Peace!

Peace, what does this word mean?
Peace is something some children have not yet seen,
A time when there is no violence, disorder or war,
Sadly, this is all some children ever saw,
A flash of lightning was a bullet out of a gun,
Peace, they've had none,
To them our world is white,
Whispers and silence just doesn't seem right,
Peace, the symbol of a dove,
Our country, surrounded by love.

Katie Denyer (14)

GROWING UP

When I was seven, I wanted to be a detective,
After each investigation I'd have tea and a digestive.

When I was eight, I wanted to be a pop star,
But singing alone was a 'Steps' too far.

When I was nine, I wanted to be a drama queen,
But I didn't have a crown for my very first scene.

When I was ten, I had hit the big one 0,
And I was allowed to meet my mates and co.

When I was eleven, I wanted to have some cats,
But I wasn't allowed them until I had done well in my SATs.

When I was twelve, I wanted a mobile phone,
But to buy it I needed a loan.

Now I'm a teenager, I'm just going to be . . .
A bored, stressy, miserable, teenager! Aarrghh!

Elizabeth Fisher (13)

MY NATURE POEM

In springtime yellow daffodils come bursting through the ground
And in the woodland glades, primroses can be found.

Tulips and forget-me-nots, harebells galore,
Primroses and daisies softly carpet the forest floor.

The trees are full of blossom,
The rosebuds' scent hangs low
And little pansies flower, and in sunlight start to grow.

Aimi Louise Mouser (13)

A Poem About Everything

Some people think the universe is everything,
Some people think their religion is everything,
Some people think that money is everything,
Some people think love is everything.

Everybody has their own view of what everything is,
There must be one meaning of everything,
Every word has a meaning, everything has a meaning,
But what is the meaning of everything?

The dictionary describes everything as:
All things of utmost importance,
But is this the true meaning of everything
Or is this just words in a dictionary contents?

So here is my answer, in my own view,
Everything has one meaning and here it is:
Everything means everything you want it to be,
Everything means everything you don't want to miss.

Everything can mean freedom, hope or joy,
Or a soulmate, you've known right from the start,
Although everything can mean money and nothing else,
Everything can mean one hug that came straight from the heart.

What I'm trying to say is everything isn't just a load of cash,
Everything can mean nothing in other people's shoes
And nothing has the complete opposite meaning to everything,
So have a think about nothing and everything and see
What you would choose.

Rebecca Laff (13)

Family And Friends

Family and friends are probably the most important people in a teenager's life,
Friends stick up for me and keep me company while
Family are always there in case I have difficulty.
But sometimes I don't need friends
Because they encourage me
To either smoke or take drugs but if I disagree they'll dump me.
My dad passed away not long ago
I felt very lonely as soon as he had to go,
School is drawing near and I can't wait,
To see the school and my classmate,
His name is Andrew Carr,
He takes my mind off everything by taking me out so very far.
Life is difficult without my dad around,
I miss him so when I look underground
He was always there for me,
In the kitchen or even on the settee,
But now I play for a footie team,
Menai Bridge Tigers are hot as steam,
We lost our friendly against Holyhead
But as soon as the season starts, we'll squash them into
Little pieces of bread.
I want to be a policeman when I am older,
My dad agreed and put his hand on my shoulder,
'I think you'll be a great policeman, son,' he said,
Even now I remember that moment clear in my head.

Barry Griffiths (14)

THE UNKNOWN

So many questions in my head
I sit there and think in my bed
I wonder what happens when we die?
Do we grow wings like angels and fly?

Is there a heaven
Or is there a hell?
Does Heaven have white curly gates
And a beautiful magic well?

I wonder where Heaven is
Somewhere out there I'm sure
Where there are rivers and streams
That run forever so pure.

How big is the universe?
Does it travel far and far?
Who made the world?
Does the maker live on a star?

Is there life on other planets?
Cabbage-like aliens who live and grow
Are we the only life out there?
I guess I'll never know.

Do such things as ghosts exist?
Do they come down from the heavens above?
How do we see them, as we want to?
Do they watch us and share our love?

Is there really a God?
Is he loyal and kind?
Why doesn't he stop the suffering?
So many questions on my mind.

Being a teenager's hard to comprehend
But make the most of life, for that's all that matters in the end.

Jackie Heath (14)

LOOKING IN FROM THE OUTSIDE

So you call this your free country?
Tell me why it costs so much to live?
How come people always take
But they rarely learn to give?

Are you happy with your life?
Would you rather be living mine?

I feel no sorrow, I feel no pain,
No one here can say the same.
Fear is not seen through these eyes,
I know not the meaning of truth or lies.

I have a superhuman mind,
I only look forward, never behind.

I live alone and learn alone
And so will die on my own.

Kate Hickmott (15)

TEENAGERS

T otally rubbish,
E veryone says, 'You've got to grow up now.'
E very mistake is yours, deliberately,
N othing I can do is right,
A ngry (most of the time).
G hastly little kids getting me in trouble,
E veryone says, 'It's your fault be more
R esponsible.' Well I'm not going to!
S o there!

Emma Allen (14)

PRESSURE

Just an eight-letter word?

Then how can it make you feel hot
And simultaneously cold,
Haze the reality of youth,
So inside you feel old?
How does it trap you in a group,
When you're inexplicably scared
And then make you steal, lie and smoke,
Along with anything else you're dared?
Why does it push you to study,
When all it does is prevent,
The clear line of thought,
Crucial for the event?
How does it change what you wear,
How you look, how you think,
Then make you pick up that bottle
And imbibe you with drink?
Once it's captured your world there's no way out,
No use in screaming, no need to shout.
All you want is to be normal, have friends and fit in,
But you don't and you cry as the knife pierces your skin.
If pressure is just an eight-letter word,
With the power to make you act against your will,
Armed with its products introspection and distrust,
Then it should be acknowledged that some words can kill!

Danielle Zandi (15)

Why Ice Cream Is The Food Of Consolation

Where relationships are hot,
Ice cream is cool.

Where lust burns,
Ice cream soothes.

Where love is bitter,
Ice cream is sweet.

Where your heart aches,
Your teeth will tingle pleasantly.

Where men may annoy your friends,
They will love ice cream.

Where men can get jealous,
Ice cream does not mind if you eat jelly too.

Where no new man's showing,
You can always buy another tub.

Where relationships are monotonous,
Ice cream has many flavours.

Where men may need special attention,
Ice cream simply requires a spoon.

Where love is confusing,
Ice cream is what it says on the label
And is always delicious too.

Elizabeth Chatterjee (15)

Where Can We Play?

Where can we go?
We want to play.
We don't know
Where we can go today.

Stick to the path,
Down in the wood,
Can we build a tree house?
We wish we could.

Down to the beach,
To play on the sand,
The hut owner comes out
And shouts, 'Get off my land.'

We play on our skateboards,
Down the Station Hill,
A man comes out and says,
'I'll report you to the Bill.'

We have a playing field,
It's OK to go there,
As long as all you do
Is just stand and stare.

We stay at home,
Playing a game,
Nowhere to go,
Every day the same.

Having a good time,
Us kids should be out,
Give us a break,
Don't just stand and shout.

Darren Pearce (14)

THROUGH TEENAGE EYES

No one understands us,
No one seems to care,
The only time they stop and look,
Is to wonder why we're there!

Our music's a little louder,
Than grown-ups usually play,
But that's just how we let it out,
After a hectic day.

School is just the worst of all,
When they put the pressure on
And we're stuck in the classroom,
Well, we'd rather be gone.

And then there's fitting in,
The most important part of all,
Cos no one wants to know you
If you're different or uncool!

Sometimes you'll get bullied,
When they try to get you down,
But if you have friends behind you,
Then there is no need to frown!

Your friends are there to help you,
They're there for when you cry
And those friends should still be with you,
Till the day you die!

Adults will never understand us,
No matter how hard each tries,
But this is how I see the world,
Through my teenage eyes.

Julie Parton (14)

THE STORM

I remember first writing your poem
All about a storm,
So maybe I'll write it again,
In a totally different form.

A whirlwind of emotions,
Floating round and round,
That's not what our life's about,
Just try to understand!

The wild storm rages
Like a fiery electronic blast
Those words come from my stereo
Ever so, ever so fast!

Then the phone rings loudly
And my mate's on the other end,
Asking what I'm up to
And if I'm out at the weekend?

I have to pick an outfit,
Whilst shopping with my pals,
To go to the greatest party,
I hope there's no rows!

And then all too soon,
The party's been and gone
And I'm getting school stuff ready,
For the term that's just begun!

So that's the end of the second storm
And the world's still turning round
Maybe there'll be another one some day
But we'll have to see for now!

Tanya Hobson (14)

INJUSTICE

I froze and faced a fearful sight.
There was nothing I could do
She lay there barely conscious,
The reason no one knew.

Her sad face was pale and washed out,
As tears ran down my cheek,
I saw my poor sister so distraught
She looked so small and weak.

I couldn't bear the whispers,
How dare they say, 'It's fake.'
More than anyone she would dread,
The uncontrollable shake!

They savagely strapped on monitors,
To see what she would do,
There seemed to be no answer,
The doctors had no clue.

She bravely battled against it
And tried to find a cure.
I supported her undoubtedly,
Her determination was pure.

Her strength of character shone,
It grew more day by day,
I know she can succeed,
She's proved it in every way.

There's no problem too big,
Or goal that's unobtainable,
Tania has shown to all of us,
That she is more than capable.

Christine Dutton (13)

THE NIGHT OF NO END

It's a cold, dark night
I think I am lost and there is no one in sight.
I travel the streets, move far and wide,
But there is no way I can escape this evil and dark side.
As my toes go numb and I can't feel my thumbs,
I wonder if someone will ever come,
As I walk the roads from end to end,
I come across a building with no end.
I decide to enter, what else could I do,
Stay outside until my legs get cold too?
As I push the door it squeaks and shrieks,
Is anyone there or is it just me?
My heart beats faster, my hands begin to shake,
Oh how I wish this nightmare could just go away.
As I become more weary and things get more scary,
I head for the corner and hurriedly take a seat,
I'm scared, I'm frightened, what should I do now?
As I bow my head and tears drop rapidly now.
Screek! Shriek! I lift my head up,
What could this be? This is just my luck,
I'm scared stiff and there's nowhere to go,
I can feel it coming closer, oh no,
I try to move, I try to lift myself up,
But there's no help there, I'm just in complete shock.
'No!' I shout, ' leave me alone,' I cry,
As it grabs my head and shakes me from side to side,
My heart beats faster, is this the end? Will I die?
As a sharp point stabs my chest
And now there is no life inside.

Danny Bwona (14)

I DON'T WANT TO GO TO SCHOOL TOMORROW

I don't want to go to school tomorrow
It will just be the same.
Every day this happens
Can't they just go away?
Leave me alone
Just for one day.

No one understands how I feel
It's hard to explain.
I look round each corner, is that him?
Maybe I'm just being insane.

I've got lunch time next
This is what I really hate
Me on my own
With just him and his mates.

I don't know what to do,
If I tell the teachers it will just make it worse,
My parents don't understand
The tormenting is just getting worse and worse.

It's just cause I'm different not the same,
Sometimes I wish I was
Then they'd let me join their game.

I don't want to go to school tomorrow
It will just be the same.
Can't they just go away?
Leave me alone,
Just for one day.

Joanna Brown (13)

TEENAGE CRUSH

From the moment I wake,
I see his face,
Till the time my eyes drift to sleep,
I hear his deep voice.

Some may call it 'love',
Some may think it's 'infatuation',
I know it's neither,
But a little, tiny teenage crush.

I would like to say hi to him one day,
I haven't got the guts to call his name,
Through I try,
All I can do is walk on by.

Maybe I'll know him,
Maybe I won't,
One day I'll say his name over the phone,
Or see it on the gravestones when we grow old.

I hope one day,
I can do the things I say,
Without having to hide these feelings inside
And go without a chance of saying goodbye.

Heather Wilson (14)

THE FUTURE

I could be a movie star,
Working on the set,
I could be a computer salesman,
Working on the Net.
Maybe I could be an astronaut,
Flying high in space,
Maybe I could be a Formula One racer,
Trying to win the race.

Maybe I could be a hairdresser
And style people's hair,
Or maybe I could be a birdwatcher
And sit all day and stare.

Samantha Perry (14)

The Rainy Day

I woke up that morning with the rain hitting off the roof,
I had never seen such rain in all my youth.
It couldn't have been coming down any faster,
Every drop looked as if it was obeying its master!
I went down the stairs and was trying to think what I could do today,
I was struggling to think of anything, as I just lay.
I watched a woman running up the street,
She was dodging all the puddles, 'cause they were that deep!
I guess my only choice was to stay in,
Which really was a sin!
Hours passed without doing anything,
I switched on the TV but that was really ming!
This weather was making me feel depressed,
I started thinking that I was obsessed!
Everyone else was away out,
But I couldn't be bothered, 'cause I was a lazy lout!
I started to study the rain,
People must have thought that I was insane!
Anyway, night-time came
And by this time I felt really lame.
I had my tea
And all this horrible weather had made me think of the sea,
I went to sleep,
Without a peep,
But then a thought came into my head,
I would've been better just staying in bed!

Katie Balmer (14)

THE WORLD IS FADING!

The world is fading far away,
From our lives each day,
Further and further it goes,
As lives are ruined constantly.

People go missing more frequently,
Many are found, but not to be alive,
Heartbreaking messages left,
With flowers that are laid.

Innocent people are afraid
For them and their loved ones,
Streets, unsafe places to be,
At morning, day or night.

People are fading far away,
From our world each day,
Further and further they go,
As time is ticking quietly.

Maya Petkovic (15)

SUMMER

Summer was here,
Now summer's gone,
Not much sunbathing,
Really got done,
The flowers grow, the gardens
Look nice,
I like to think that colour
Adds spice,
Soon the clouds come over grey
Everyone moans, 'No sun today.'

Leanne Huntley (13)

WHY?

Why is the world forever at war?
With thousands who are hungry, homeless and poor?
Why can't we try to live in peace
Or to be civil to one another at least?

Why can't they cancel third-world debt?
It's not their problem, they'd rather forget.
Why are there people who murder and abuse?
Is it so they're the topic of the morning news?

Why do some people have such a perfect life?
While others long for justice, or just a day without strife?
Why is the world full of sadness and grief?
We'll never know the answers, all we have is belief . . .

. . . that people make bad things happen will feel compassion and love
And make a change for the better with the help of the powers
from above.

Claire Keegan (15)

PATCHWORK FAMILY

The original sheet was irreparable,
The material thin and the stitches undone,
So the sheet was cut up, the patches separated
And new patches were introduced,
To make the sheet whole again.
Some of the patches did not match,
The patterns too different,
So they were discarded
And many other patches after them,
Until the right colours were discovered, tested
And stitched carefully in with the patches of the old sheet,
For a patchwork family.

Ceri Pedrick (15)

Being a Teenager

For me being a teenager is like a chapter in a book
Spotty face, annoying siblings and always worrying about your looks.
Gossiping with my friends about who's dating who,
Staring at the gorgeous boys, which is nothing new!

It is always tough in the morning to leave my bed,
Getting ready to go that place all teenagers dread,
That place we call school, which is such a bore,
Giving us pointless homework, which is more like a chore.

Parents thinking you're a roller coaster ride,
Calm like a sunny day or up and down like a tide,
Sad one minute and driving them up the wall,
Happy the next, when you get that important phone call.

Being a teenager . . . well there's nothing much to tell,
Sometimes it can be heaven and sometimes it can be hell.

Eva Owusu-Ansah (15)

Disabled in Her Own World

What is she thinking?
How does she feel?
What's going on in her head?
She always seems happy,
But sometimes confused?
Does she understand all that's been said?

She can be scared,
She can be happy,
But she still doesn't understand,
She gives you kisses,
She gives you cuddles,
She always wants to hold your hand.

She is very mysterious,
She is very friendly,
But life isn't always bliss,
She can be annoying,
She can be upsetting,
But overall I'm glad she's my sis!

Janine Dunn (13)

THE WAIT

Sitting, waiting, anticipating,
Nerves beginning to set in.
I think that when they come through the door,
I'll throw them in the bin!

I look at my watch, it's half-past seven,
Only thirty minutes more.
I can't believe in half an hour,
They'll be lying on my floor!

It's ten to eight, I'm so nervous,
I'm strolling up and down.
I tell myself I'll be OK
And remember not to frown.

I watch the letterbox with baited breath,
It's my gateway to pass or fail.
All of a sudden, without a blink of an eye,
Someone pushes through the mail!

On no! They're here, what shall I do?
This is a moment I'll never forget.
I slowly open my exam results,
I wonder what I'll get?

Craig Martin (15)

Sweet Child Of Mine

You came into our lives like an unplanned sunrise,
Stealing our time, our patience was tried.
You demanded, you protested, you got your own way,
For a minute of madness, we made you pay.

Bundled and wrapped and placed in a cot,
For a short time in your life you knew us now.
But now you have grown and at last speak your mind,
Your true loving place, God will find.

Remember in your heart that we did what was best,
And that leaving you alone, left us sleepless, without rest,
We had our own lives and we were so young
And the life you had, had only just begun.

We hope our little guidance helped for a while
And that you remember your parents, our sweet child,
Do not feel abandoned, as our love goes on,
Throughout your life and chapters beyond.

Claire Reed (14)

A Day Like This . . .

You know one of those days when the wind blows
Softly in through the window,
Days when your mind drifts away somewhere where
Your body can't go,
A day when you sit and watch the clouds float by
And in the distance you can hear a gentle bird cry.

Your ears and eyes block out the world,
The colours of life are mixed and swirled,
It feels like you could fall into the sky,
As you watch the timid dragonfly.

A day when as soon as the sun rises it sets
And it seems like you could catch the sun with fishing nets,
You can do everything and nothing all at once,
You don't want one day, you want months.

A day when nothing is everything and everything is nothing . . .

Elizabeth Eaglen (14)

ENEMIES

Like vultures they stand there
watching and waiting
watching and waiting
for your next mistake.
Like leeches they sit there
Sucking and feeding
Sucking and feeding
On your last mistake.
Like lions they prowl in packs
Stuck up and proud
Stuck up and proud
Thinking they're 'it'
But like a caterpillar I creep
Waiting for a chance
To gain power over them
So I can spread my wings and become
The most magnificent and beautiful of all.
I will fly high
And show them their
Watching and waiting
Sucking and feeding
Won't keep me down.

Amie Stanley (15)

TIME

Look at where we are and
Where we have been to,
Time to share our dreams
And fears.

Time is every day, every hour
And every second,
Telling our past, our future
And our present.

Enjoy every moment of
Our spare time,
Share it with friends and families
Who we love and care for.

Time takes us from dusk to dawn,
As precious as it can be.

Time goes on and on,
Every day,
Like the pulse of our
Heart beating.

Liezl Ann Orenzo (15)

ME AND HER

As I saw her for the first time, she looked like an angel,
that had lost her way. With her eyes as green as the grass
she was walking on. Her hair was long and blonde, that was so shiny
that it would reflect the sun off it.

The most beautiful thing about her was her smile,
her lips were bright red and her teeth were like the moon in
the dark night, bright and beautiful.

All I could do was just look at her because if I said a word, she would be like a butterfly, beautiful but if you were too loud or move too quickly, she would become scared, fly away and never be seen again. All I did was look at her And spared the moment and that was my special moment.

Joshua Jones (15)

NOBODY KNOWS MY TRUE FACE . . .

Nobody knows my true face
I look in the mirror
And the smile I see
Is not mine.

I walk to the place we meet
I see you there
And the laugh I hear
Is untrue.

I'm a good actress
Aren't I?
I fooled you
You thought this was real.

I wish I could just
Be myself
Be who I want
And be happy.

Instead I have lies and charades
Fake emotions
And I wish
I could be free.

Nobody knows my true face . . .

Hannah Dickson (14)

Best Friends!

If I die before you do
I'll go to Heaven and wait for you
And when you come and see me there,
I'll let you know how much I care.
For all the days we've spent together,
I've hoped our friendship lasts forever.
The tears we've cried,
From all the laughs we've had,
We never once felt lonely and sad.
I'll remember you
And you'll remember me,
Best friends is what we'll always be!

Nicolle Green (15)

Life

Emotions get bottled up,
At school, at home,
Being a teen is not all it is said to be,
You may have a good time,
Make new friends,
You may want to cry,
Things get on top of you,
Suddenly you snap and let go,
Tears in your eyes,
Blocked up nose,
The worries are gone,
Till next time!

Emma Hatton (14)

IT AIN'T WHAT YOU DO - IT'S WHAT IT DOES TO YOU

I have not been in an eight-storey mansion
With luscious green gardens
Where every Sunday you sit and read the newspaper
With a glazing, red-hot glowing fire for comfort.

But I have been to a place where people's bare feet
Are blistered from the hot naked ground,
Houses made of iron sheets, newspaper used as decoration.

I have not been to a school where race is an issue,
Where children don't have choices.

But I have been to a school where children are
Killed for wanting to be taught in their mother tongue
Where church has been turned into a bloodbath,
Feeling your friend's blood cover you as she is shot to death.

I have held, close to my heart, a child of two diagnosed with AIDS,
He will die, and knowing the tightness in your throat and the tears
You cry won't let him live,
To see the things I've seen that feeling, I feel
I pray to God you never know.

Amy Cammidge (15)

OUR WORLD TODAY

In our world we have day and night,
Angry people and teenage fights,
Underage drinking and too many drugs,
There's no more love and no more hugs.
Why has everything gone this way?
I liked it before, why couldn't it stay?

Lindsay Alderson (14)

I Love You

My life is so perfect having you by my side,
When I see you, I can't help but smile
And I can't help but gaze lovingly into your deep green eyes,
As the love I hold for you, is never going to die.

I love you so much I really do,
More than I could possibly say
And my love for you grows stronger every day,
You've made my heart and life whole,
But most importantly . . . my soul.

I can't stop thinking about you.
I can't stop dreaming about you.
I want to hold you close, touch you, kiss you
And tell you with all of my heart that *I love you.*

I've never been so happy,
I've never smiled so much,
I've never felt so whole
And I've never loved anyone the way I love you.

I gave you my heart and in return you gave me yours,
You gave me your soul and in return I gave you mine.
I feel as though we've been together forever
And I know this feeling will always last.
I hope you realise how much you mean to me,
Because I'm never going to let you go.

I love you!

Lesley Ann Skipper (16)